Sober.House.

(My Story)

Mallory Neuberger

PAGE PUBLISHING, INC.
New York, NY

First originally published by Page Publishing, Inc. 2019

This book is a memoir based on a true story. The only characters who have given permission for their real names to be used are Mallory Neuberger, Mark Neuberger, and Mallory's children Morgan and Jack. All other characters have been fictionalized to protect their identity. Any similarities to other real people are coincidental.

ISBN 978-1-64462-393-0 (Paperback)
ISBN 978-1-64462-396-1 (Digital)

Printed in the United States of America

This book is dedicated to my mother and all the other people who never found recovery.

Contents

Part 3: Sober House

Epilogue

Foreword

When asked to write the foreword for Mallory's book, to say I was honored would be an understatement. As a licensed clinician working in the field of addiction for twenty years, I have come in contact with countless treatment centers, halfway houses, sober homes, clinicians, case managers, sober coaches, etc. As has been publicized most recently in South Florida, the professional integrity of the field has become increasingly compromised by some. The ability to find trust and work with those who have compassion, understanding, and truly passionate about the fight against the disease of addiction has become more and more difficult. I am so proud and blessed to say this is not the case with Mallory and her work.

Mallory is a woman who has dedicated and continues to dedicate her life to the women she works with. She is forever involved and hyperaware of how vulnerable these women can be in early recovery. In a time where there are some who would take advantage and exploit this vulnerability, Mallory's mission is to protect it. She is firm and fair, understanding the need of fostering independence while also providing consistent guidance. Mallory provides not only a house for women in recovery but also a home. The women join together in solidarity supporting one another, reflective of the mission of The Frog Pad. This is an environment that creates a safe space for women to heal and to grow. I am grateful for those in the industry like Mallory who uphold their integrity, convey their passion, and have an authentic care for those who are caught in the life-threatening battle of addiction.

Jennifer Lorey, LCSW, CEDS,

psychotherapist, Boca Raton, Florida

Previously clinical director of Florida House Experience

Preface

I opened the doors of my first sober house in February 2015. Books about addiction and recovery have always been some of my favorites—in particular, *A Million Little Pieces* by James Frey, and *Beautiful Boy* and *Tweak* by David Sheff and Nic Sheff (father and son), describing how addiction impacts not only the addict but also the family.

So far, I haven't come across any books written about sober houses, which are also called recovery houses and halfway houses. These homes play a very important role for many people in recovery, helping them move from early sobriety into living a sober life in the outside world. I felt that reading about this could help many people.

A sober house is a bridge back to the outside world. Many residents move in after completing inpatient treatment. They still aren't ready to be completely independent, so they choose a sober house with structure and accountability. Sometimes they don't trust themselves—and often their friends and family aren't ready to have them back.

During one's stay at a sober house, the resident will attend 12-step meetings, find sponsors, and hopefully, form relationships with other people in recovery. They will be tested for alcohol and drugs regularly. They will tiptoe back into the real world with the support of their peers and staff. Many will begin to work or volunteer—their days will be structured and safe. They will depart when they have a good foundation in recovery with the tools necessary to live sober and productive lives.

Sober houses have a very bad reputation in many areas, because not everybody who opens them has good motives. Some people are exploiting addicts and their loved ones, which has resulted in a lot of negative press. For those of us, like me, who are truly trying to make a positive difference in the lives of recovering addicts, there are some wonderful houses available.

This is my story of addiction, recovery, and running sober houses in Florida in order to pay back to the world of addiction and recovery for the amazing life it has offered me.

Acknowledgments

Thank you to my early readers: Lorrie Mackain, Ellen Fagan, Todd Greenberg, and Ilene and Bernie Shaiken.

Thanks to The Writers Colony in Delray Beach, Florida, for providing me with the push I needed to get this started and for your encouragement as my writing progressed.

Thank you to my husband, Mark, who put up with my writing at all hours of the day and night. I could not have achieved this without your support.

And especially, thank you to my patient teacher and editor, Barbara Cronie. You created order and provided proper punctuation.

One pill makes you larger, and one pill makes you small

And the ones that mother gives you, don't do anything at all

Go ask Alice, when she's ten feet tall.

—White Rabbit, Jefferson Airplane

It's because, of these drugs, that I do, that make me

Do these things, that I do, do these things, that I do.

—These Drugs, Eminem

Humpty Dumpty sat on a wall,

Humpty Dumpty had a great fall;

All the king's horses and all the king's men

Couldn't put Humpty together again.

—English Nursery Rhyme

Addiction

How Could I Be a Drug Addict?

Sitting in business class on the plane, flying back to JFK International from Greece, I couldn't wait to call my drug dealer. I hadn't snorted coke in days, or weeks even, so clearly I wasn't an addict. If I were an addict, I wouldn't have been able to function without coke for almost three weeks. Right?

I looked at myself in my magnifying hand mirror. I had a rich, glowing tan that made my brown eyes look lighter. My dark hair had lighter highlights from weeks in the Mediterranean summer sun. I put some light pink lip gloss on my already-pink lips and smiled at myself. *Looking good*, I thought. Thin. Tan. Healthy and well rested. Not bad for fifty.

Waiting at customs, I saw the signs that stated No Cell Phone Use, but I didn't care. I had a call to make—a very important call.

"What are you doing?" my husband, Mark, asked. "It says 'No Cell Phones.' You're going to get arrested."

"Oh, stop it," I replied with irritation in my voice. "I am not going to get arrested."

"Who are you calling anyway?" he wanted to know.

"Nobody. Just worry about yourself and leave me alone."

One of the things that made Mark a good husband for me was that he believed whatever I told him. He had no idea that I snorted coke, and we had been together for a couple of years already. It was easy to just act annoyed or ignore him, and he never really called me out on my strange behaviors. I could leave parties, restaurants, or family dinners for a half hour at a time, and he would hardly notice that I had been gone. A simple excuse (I had to go to the bathroom, or my daughter needed to speak to me) always sufficed.

The call went into voice mail, and I left a message: "I'm back! When can you come by?"

Just hearing his voice message filled me with anticipation. I could already feel that first hit going up my nose, filling my body with relief, with relaxation, with joy. I would only do two hits tonight when he met me. Two hits, and I would save the rest for tomorrow. It was late already, and I couldn't afford to be up all night. I had to work tomorrow, pick my son up at school, unpack, buy groceries, and make dinner.

Finally, my dealer, Carl, texted me, *You around?*

I'll be home in less than an hour.

Call me when you're home, my dealer replied.

He didn't like waiting. He was a busy man with many stops to make.

I'll be home in fifteen minutes, I texted him as our driver paid the toll at the Holland Tunnel. *You nearby?*

An hour, he wrote back.

I knew I should tell him no. It was already 10:00 p.m. I needed to sleep, to prevent jet lag.

Great, I wrote. *See you soon!*

"Who are you texting?" Mark asked.

"Work stuff for tomorrow," I replied. This wasn't going to be easy. I needed an excuse to leave the apartment an hour after we got home. My husband would be suspicious, but that had never stopped me before.

Mark truly had no idea that I did drugs. Nobody really knew, other than my dealer and a few friends who still partook with me. Snorting cocaine at the age of fifty was not really something that I was publicizing. The cool party days had ended a long time ago. If people knew I was doing this, they might make me stop. So I protected my drug use carefully. I didn't want to stop and didn't particularly want to share. It was better this way. Mark just knew that I could stay up really late with him and I was a good party partner. This was a quality he had very much been looking for in a second wife, and I was the perfect candidate with my secret addiction. Without it, I would be in bed at nine every night like his ex-wife.

Snorting coke kept me nice and thin. I liked showing off my supertoned stomach in my size 27 jeans, which were so loose that I could pull them up and down without unzipping or unsnapping them. Not many fifty-year-olds that I knew looked as buff as me, and I liked the attention people gave me when I lifted my shirt in bars and restaurants or at parties.

Finally arriving at our Soho loft after what felt like an interminable drive, I texted my dealer as Mark unlocked our front door. I unpacked a few things, sorted through some mail, and checked my e-mails. I couldn't wait for my dealer to text me back.

My cell phone rang, scaring me half to death. "Be on the corner of Spring and Greenwich in five minutes," he said. It was 11:03 p.m.

"Ok," I promised. I almost always bought the same thing, so he knew what I wanted unless I specified otherwise. We didn't discuss these things on the phone. He had spent several years in prison for dealing before, so he had to be very careful. Sometimes I envisioned us getting busted by the cops as we did our little swap, me ending up in the papers like Tatum O'Neal when she was arrested while buying cocaine not far from where we lived. The thought filled me with horror, but there was also a strange, illicit excitement to the exchange.

"Who was that?" Mark asked.

"Nobody," I said, running out the door, money in my pocket, a straw already cut with the longer end hidden in the trash under some junk mail. "I'll be right back."

I walked to the corner, and Carl pulled up on a little motor scooter a few minutes later. Sometimes he was on scooters, other times in nondescript rental cars.

"Looking good, babes," he said, kissing me on both cheeks. "Long time no see." He put his helmet down on the scooter seat where I knew my package would be sitting inside. I scooped it up and put it in the back pocket of my jeans, depositing the cash in its place.

I stood up straight and lifted one leg up, showing off my new Gucci sandals, their three-inch heels adding to my already-statuesque five-foot-seven-inch frame. I sucked in my stomach a little, wanting to look especially fit and stylish. Why was I trying to impress my drug dealer? Probably so he would come back the next time I called him, possibly putting me ahead of less charming customers.

"See you soon," I told him. I walked around the back of my building and took the little package from my back pocket, placing it in my left hand. I snorted into my right nostril and then switched the bag to my other hand, evening out the left side of my nose. *God, that felt good!* I walked back into my apartment and locked the door behind me.

"Where were you?" Mark asked.

"I just had to make a phone call. I needed a little privacy."

I went into the bathroom and locked the door behind me, opening my little package again. The next time I looked at the clock, it was 4:00 a.m. So good to be home.

How I Started and How I Couldn't Stop

That first hit was always the best, bringing me back to the very first time I was introduced to coke. I had never been as terrified or as excited as I was that afternoon. I knew that what we were doing was very bad, which made it seem particularly alluring.

I had smoked weed and hash since the age of twelve, and that already bored me, making me paranoid, giving me cottonmouth, and turning my eyes a very bright red. Drinking was something that I did when I was out with my friends, but I didn't have a real taste for it. My preferred cocktails were apricot sours, sloe gin fizzes, and tequila sunrises—basically anything that looked pretty and didn't taste of alcohol at all. One or two of those, and I was toasted for the night.

The only time I got drunk was the year before I tried coke. I was a junior in high school in Port Washington, a Long Island suburb. My friend Barbara and I had gone out with two boys who were in their senior year. They had a bottle of vodka and a bottle of 7-Up in their car. My first sip of the mixed drink was not to my liking, so I poured a full plastic cup full of straight vodka and drank it right down, holding the cup with my right hand and my nose with my left. I took a swig of 7-Up as a chaser.

That was the last thing I remembered. I woke up lying on the tiles outside my front door, the burglar alarm blaring. My father emerged in his bathrobe, unlocking the door to the mudroom, and saw me covered in vomit, my adorable denim halter dress no longer fresh and innocently sexy. Our bichons frises started licking the vomit off me and barking up a storm, excited by this late-night interruption.

"I'm so sorry, Mr. Grayson," Barbara said, my key dangling from her hand. "Mallory just had a little bit too much to drink, and I was trying to unlock the door for her."

I felt like death the next morning, my head pounding and my entire body feeling as if I had been beaten up in a street fight. Clearly, drinking was not for me. I vowed to myself that in the future I would drink like a lady for social reasons only. My father was sweet, phoning me from work and asking me how I felt.

"Not so good, Daddy," I admitted, tears welling up in my eyes.

My father laughed. "You never listen… You always have to try things for yourself. Feel better, sweetheart."

The first time I did cocaine, I had just turned seventeen years old. I was a senior in high school, and one of my friends had a "dime bag," which was essentially ten dollars' worth of coke. This was a very small amount, especially when you take into account that four of us were sharing it.

Only Claudine, the girl who purchased it, had ever tried it before. She had an older sister who introduced her to it. My other two friends, Susan and Lynn, were novices like me. We sat in a circle on Claudine's bedroom floor. Both of her parents worked, and it was just the four of us in her house, hanging out on a Friday afternoon after school.

Claudine had a big mirror in front of her on the floor, and she poured the cocaine onto the center of it. It had been packed in a small white paper package, the paper glossy and specially folded like a tiny envelope. She had a straight razor and scraped the remaining white powder from the paper, letting it sprinkle on top of the small pile that already rested there.

I was enthralled. I loved the mirror, the little envelope, and the razor blade. A twenty-dollar bill sat beside the mirror, waiting to be rolled up into a straw.

Claudine chopped the already-fine powder with the pointed edge of the razor blade. Once she had chopped it for what felt like forever, she began to cut the powder into thin white lines, their shadows reflected in the mirror. There were eight lines in total—two for each of us. Claudine intricately rolled the twenty-dollar bill to look like a straw by folding one corner down into a little triangle and then rolling the bill the other way, nice and tight, until she could slip the money into the little catch she had made, securing it closed.

Lynn and Susan looked as enthralled as I felt. We all drank on weekends and had smoked pot and hash before, but this was a first for the three of us.

"Who's first?" Claudine asked, looking around the circle. I didn't want to go first since I didn't know what to do, so I sat quietly. Lynn and Susan must have felt the same way, because they didn't offer to try it first either.

"Okay, then," Claudine said, looking at all three of us. "I'll go first."

She seemed very adult to me that afternoon. She had secured an empty house, purchased a new and very illicit drug for us to try, and knew how to use it. At times like this, I wished that I had a cool older sister like hers.

Claudine had superlong blond hair, but it was frizzy, which was not the style. The rest of us worked very hard to get our hair straight each morning, regardless of the weather. I wore my long brown hair in a loose ponytail on top of my head every night, clipped down in the back with a barrette, ensuring the sleekest results when I woke up. It wasn't comfortable, but being an attractive girl came at a price, even at seventeen.

Claudine had beautiful blue eyes, but her big bumpy nose detracted from their beauty. She bent her head down, and Susan went behind her to hold her hair back, keeping it from falling onto the mirror and disrupting our precious little stash. She put the twenty-dollar-bill straw into one of her nostrils and snorted half of one of the tiny lines. Then she switched the straw to her other nostril and finished it up.

She handed the straw to Lynn, who did the same, while Susan held her dark brown hair back. Susan had become the official hair holder, and she moved to me next, pulling my hair back into her hands. I bent down to the mirror and saw myself looking back. My brown eyes looked bigger than ever, filled with curiosity and excitement. I put the makeshift straw into my right nostril and held my left nostril in with my left index finger like I had seen Claudine do. I inhaled, and the powder exploded into my head, seeming to go directly to my brain. I moved the straw to the left and repeated the gesture. My head felt amazingly clear, everything around me suddenly brighter and more intense.

We continued our little rituals until each of us had snorted our two lines and were out of coke.

"I need a cigarette," Claudine announced.

With an echo of "Me too," we all got out our assorted brands from our purses: Newport Lights, Parliament, True Blue, and Camel. We went outside to our normal smoking spot in her backyard and puffed away.

I loved cocaine from the minute we sat down around that mirror. I loved the "badness" of it, the process of cutting it up, the feeling of it going up my nose. I couldn't wait to do it again.

I had started smoking hash and pot when I was twelve, and by seventeen, I didn't like it any more. It made my eyes super-red and my mouth cottony dry. Pot made me para-noid and self-conscious. It also gave me the munchies, and I didn't want to get fat eating countless Oreos.

Cocaine was my "it" drug. I loved it like an unattain-able man—I chased it, savored it, and thought of it con-stantly. Almost from the very beginning, it had me in its claws. If it was there, I wanted it, and if there was more of it, I didn't want to stop. It was a problem from the very beginning.

Freshman year of college, my new friend Avery intro-duced me to two senior boys. A cute small girl, Avery drank Jim Beam like a man and laughed at my white wine spritzers, which had become one of my drink staples.

"Don and Chris invited us to their house," Avery said right before last call one night at our college bar. "They have coke."

I hadn't done coke again since my initial introduction, and I felt my heart speed up in anticipation. *Coke! Yay!* I could already taste the sour drip down the back of my throat, could clearly imagine the immediate clarity of my senses as soon as that first hit entered my nose and spread throughout my body.

The guys had an off-campus house right near the bar, and we walked over in a foot of snow. Once we had taken off our boots, coats, hats, and gloves, we sat around a coffee table in their living room. They passed out beers, and Chris got to work on the coke. He had taken a framed picture off the wall and was pouring a big pile of white powder out onto the glass that covered it. There was probably five times the amount on the picture than I had tried with my high school friends, and the plastic bag that he poured from had lots more inside.

"Have you ever tried this before, Mallory?" Chris asked. He was a big, preppy Main Line guy—clearly the product of prep school, with his well-worn chinos and his rag wool sweater.

"Yes," I told him boldly, smiling a little.

"Well, let's see how you girls handle this," he said, pushing the picture toward Avery and me. I picked up the rolled bill—a hundred this time—and snorted half of a big line on the right side, the other half on the left. I felt relief immediately—immense joy and happiness.

"Wow!" Don said. "She's a pro. Do another one."

So I did, and then handed the straw to Avery, who did the same.

Hours later, Avery and I trudged up the hill to our all women's dorm. The sun was up, glistening against the snow, which was everywhere. We had stayed up all night, doing coke, listening to music, drinking beer, and smoking cigarettes.

Filled with guilt, I felt sick to my stomach. *What would my parents think if they could see me now? They would be so disappointed in me.* These shameful thoughts followed me for the next seventeen years. I dated guys who snorted cocaine. I dated guys who sold cocaine. I bought cocaine. I snorted cocaine.

I could go long stretches without the drug. Out of sight, out of mind. There were nights where I flushed my remaining supply down the toilet because otherwise I couldn't stop myself from snorting more, regardless of what the next day held in store. Many of the people I hung out with were worse than me, so they didn't see anything wrong with what I was doing. I had a group of girlfriends who loved the same things as me.

"Chardonnay, *s'il vous plaît.*" We laughed as we ordered in restaurants. We would snort some lines before going out, and then drink wine for hours in bars and restaurants, before going home to do some more lines.

"I'll have the french fries and the goat cheese salad with Dijon mustard, please," I told my servers at restaurants in Greenwich Village, Beverly Hills, and Aspen.

"Me too," my friends would echo.

Our food would arrive, and we would take a bite or two. "These are *the best* french fries anywhere," we would exclaim to one another. Watching our weight was not an issue. Our primary food source was the grapes that had been crushed into chardonnay, so we could afford to splurge on a few fries and random forkfuls of goat cheese salad.

Family Ties

My birth family was never very close, and friends became my family from a very young age. Given the choice, I preferred to stay in my room and talk on the phone or hang out with my peers rather than my own family. I didn't feel much love or acceptance at home, so I looked outside for affirmation. This resulted in a lot of friendships and countless relationships with guys.

"I love you, but I don't like you!" my parents would tell me often as a child. I didn't understand how my own parents couldn't like me, but they found me to be particularly awful. Many of my friends had amazing parents who would do anything for their children, and I wondered why my parents weren't the same with me.

"Hi, Daddy!" I yelled every night as soon as I heard my dad walk in through the garage door. I was excited to share my latest news with him, and handed him his drink and then threw my arms around his legs. He taught me how to make a very dry gin martini by the time I was six years old. I would pour the Tanqueray and pretend to pour some vermouth on top (that was "very dry," I was told) and present it to him when he walked through the playroom door.

"Goddamn it, Mallory!" my father would say. "Can't I even take my shoes off before you start in with me?" I would walk to my room, dejected, sometimes crying myself to sleep. The smell of gin soothed me, reminding me of my beautiful father, the man I wanted nothing more from than unconditional love.

In the back seat of our family car, wedged in between my two brothers, I chattered away.

"If you don't talk for the rest of the ride home, I'll pay you a dime," my mother told me. *What? Why don't they want to hear what I'm saying?* "It's not worth it for a dime."

"I'll add a quarter," my dad added.

"And I'll put in another dime," my older brother said.

"Okay," I said sadly.

All the way to our destination I sat quietly, dying to speak, but wanting the money. Right before we arrived, my older brother Jay began to hound me until I eventually had to say something. He was three years older than me and the king of manipulating me. I didn't collect the money and went to my room crying, feeling uncared for and stupid.

At night, I lay in bed sobbing, knowing that my mother could hear me through our shared wall. I could hear her, so surely she heard my cries for help. I was afraid that I had cancer or leukemia, and I had trouble falling asleep. Sometimes my legs felt strange, something I came to learn later was called Restless Leg Syndrome.

Other people seemed to like me, so I spent as much time outside the house or locked away in my room as possible. I had lots of friends, and I tended to attract a lot of people who were especially broken and needy. They would open up and confide in me immediately, causing me to feel as if we were kindred spirits. Often they became clingy and overly demanding of my time and attention. Being needed held a lot of appeal for me, and I reveled in the attention. I loved helping people sort out their problems and felt like I was able to impart good advice and listening ears.

When my little brother, Brett, was born, four years after me, I focused my family time on him. When he cried, I ran to help him. "Do you want a bottle?" I brought him a bottle. "Do you want to play?" If he stopped crying, I climbed into his crib to play with him.

Brett didn't learn to speak the way Jay and I had. By the age of four, he hadn't uttered a single word.

"Brett doesn't need to speak," my mother told the speech pathologist. "Mallory does everything for him."

Every week, I rode in the car with my mother to pick Brett up from speech therapy. He would run into the car, holding fists full of candy. I felt bad that Brett couldn't talk, especially since it was my fault. I tried to make him speak his words when he wanted something, and when he was old enough, I devised a method of teaching him how to read. We sat together for hours, a picture book between us, as I pointed out words to him.

"The," he said when I pointed to an underlined word.

"And," he said when I pointed to a circled word.

"Good boy!" I told him. "You're reading!" He would smile, proud to be a part of my game. He was so adorable, and the only person in my nuclear family who made me feel loved. Just seeing me put a smile on his beautiful little face, and his happiness made me feel appreciated and complete. As he got older though, he locked himself in his room, keeping me away.

I had little bumps all over my arms and legs growing up. I picked at these bumps for hours, causing them to bleed and swell. "You'll grow out of them," my pediatrician promised. "They should be gone by the time you're twelve." They weren't though, and I couldn't keep my nails off them.

"Stop picking," Jay told me when I showed him my mangled legs and arms. "You're just making it worse."

"You have a heat rash," the other girls at camp told me. I knew that it wasn't a heat rash, but I was ashamed of my bumps and felt sorry for myself. The worse I felt, the more I picked. *Why can't I have smooth skin like other kids?*

Friends of mine snacked on junk food and never gained weight, while I ate carrots and drank Tab. *Why can't I be naturally thin like other kids? Why can't I be smarter, thinner, prettier, better?*

I Suck Anyway, so Why Bother Trying?

Growing up, I thought that I sucked at everything. My older brother, Jay, was perfect in every way, and as his younger sister, I couldn't keep up. Jay excelled at sports—particularly tennis. He was also the perfect student. Jay would memorize facts from the *Guinness Book of World Records*, and then he would bet me everything I had—my allowance, my Beatles albums. I was always wrong, and he was always right. He won everything that mattered to me.

Growing up in Jay's shadow, I knew that I couldn't compete, so I never bothered trying. When I entered a classroom that he had been in, teachers sometimes asked me if I was Jay's younger sister.

"No, I'm not," I answered, looking them right in the eye. "I don't have an older brother." *I'm not admitting to that. If they know I'm Jay's sister, they'll expect me to be as smart as he is.* I didn't want to be compared, because I was certain that I would fall short.

In high school I tried to exercise, wanting to be as thin as my friends. When Jay was home from college and we went running, he would pass me saying, "You're not a very fast runner, Mallory." *Why doesn't he just run ahead? Why does he always have to tell me how bad I am at everything?*

The one thing I was good at was making friends. In Great Neck, Long Island, I felt that popularity was everything. I was more popular than Jay was, so I focused on my friends. During junior high school at Great Neck North, instead of trying to do well in school, I smoked pot at lunchtime, and just sat through my classes afterward, daydreaming about outfits I wanted, cute boys, and parties I had been invited to. While Jay was playing tennis and lacrosse after school, I was hanging out with my friends. While he was doing homework and playing his guitar, I was smoking cigarettes and stealing from stores in town. I took piano lessons, but nobody in my family wanted to listen to me practice, so I only played during my weekly lessons.

Even when I skipped third grade, I thought I was stupid. When I was unprepared for a math test one day, I stole the test from my teacher's desk when she stepped outside the classroom. Everyone had seen me take it, and I felt empowered.

"Where's my test?" the teacher asked when she returned to the classroom. "Give it to me right now!"

She looked around the room, and her eyes rested on me. The test was in my desk, and I quickly slipped it into my handbag when she looked away.

Our teacher was skinny and nervous, and I loved riling her up. I sucked at math. I never paid attention, so as the lessons progressed, I was completely clueless. I knew I would fail if I took it.

The teacher walked over to my desk and stood above me. "Give me the test, Mallory!" she said. The veins in her skinny forehead were protruding, and her pale skin was red and blotchy. "I know you have it!"

I just stared her in the eyes. "No, I don't."

She opened my desk and looked inside, pushing my papers around.

"Give me your handbag!" she said. "I know it's in there."

"You have no right to inspect my personal belongings," I replied glibly.

The teacher tried to grab my bag, and I held it tightly to my chest, refusing to hand it over. She sent me to the principal's office, where I was asked to sit outside for the rest of the day. Everyone looked at me as they walked by, and I smiled at each of them, proud for pulling my stunt off. I sat outside that office frequently, falling even further behind in the subjects that I disliked. I was sent to detention sometimes, where I sat with the other dumb troublemakers. I liked being rebellious, and detention forced me to do the little homework that I was assigned.

As a young girl, I was obsessed with the *Little Miss America* pageant. I would sit glued to the TV, watching my peers dressing up in pretty clothes, strutting down the runway. They played the piano or danced ballet. *I want to be Little Miss America.*

My mother was also a big fan of the beauty pageants, and whenever we watched them together, she cried when the winner was crowned. *When I win,* I thought, *she's going to cry for me. I'm going to make her so proud.*

"Mommy," I finally told her, "I want to be Little Miss America."

"But you don't have a talent."

I did have talent. I knew I did. I could play "Fur Elise" on the piano. I was also an archery champion at summer camp. Every year, I was named the best archer in camp. I could get a bull's-eye every time I shot an arrow. I walked around all summer sporting the Maid Marion award, attesting to my excellence in archery. It was a small beaded necklace, and I wore it proudly. Team sports were never my thing, and despite my popularity, I was always one of the last girls chosen for a team. I liked singular sports—swimming and archery. My first summer away, my parents insisted that the camp staff let me swim the lake. I was six years old, the youngest camper who had ever been allowed to cross.

"Archery isn't a sport," my father told me when I explained that I wanted to compete nationally.

I Want to Help You

Many of my earliest memories involve people who were broken in some way. I was fascinated by illness, misfortune, physical and mental disabilities, death, and suffering. I was too young to understand or articulate my interests, but I studied things from afar and read as many books as I could find to shed light on my mild obsession.

Leah, an unpopular girl my age who lived on our street in Great Neck, had a dad who suffered from polio. He had a skinny leg that was covered in a big metal brace. He limped when he walked. I spent lots of time with Leah when we were nine years old. I was afraid of her father—the results of his illness were so disfiguring—but I didn't think his children deserved to be shunned due to something that was not their fault. I was relieved that my parents weren't like that. My mother assured me that I couldn't catch the polio that had disfigured Leah's father years earlier, so I visited their home regularly, even sleeping over sometimes. I was always scared when I visited, slightly nauseated but sure to be polite and helpful.

There were thalidomide children in our town. I saw one at school—he had tiny hands protruding from his shoulders, fingers not counting up to five. Other children walked away from this boy, steering clear from him as if he had chosen to be born this way, as if he were contagious. I learned from my mother that a morning sickness drug that many women had taken during their pregnancies had resulted in this disorder. The drug came from Germany and hadn't been approved in the United States. I knew that my parents traveled to Europe often, and I feared that I might get thalidomide too.

"Did you ever take it, Mommy?"

"No, thank God," my mother replied, a long plume of cigarette smoke escaping her nostrils and mouth simultaneously, "but I have a friend who did. It's a good thing we weren't in Germany, because I had terrible nausea with you and your brothers, and I probably would have taken it."

Some nights I lay in bed—unable to sleep—thinking about thalidomide, polio, leukemia, kidnappers, killer dogs. My legs would feel nervous, making it even harder to settle down. When the Jerry Lewis telethon aired on television each year, I watched the children with cerebral palsy on the small yellow Sony television in my bedroom, calling the number they provided to donate my allowance to help find a cure. The show gave me nightmares, but I couldn't tear myself away from it, hour after hour, year after year.

I was obsessed with Helen Keller. She had been blinded and deafened as a direct result of having scarlet fever. I had suffered from scarlet fever too, breaking out in fever and a terrible red rash when I was nine years old. When the doctor gave us my diagnosis, I was petrified.

"Am I going to be blind and deaf like Helen Keller?" I asked him. Tears were filling my eyes, as much from fear as from sickness.

"Of course not. We have penicillin now to cure scarlet fever."

I reminded my mother to give me my penicillin every day, worried that I would become blind and deaf if I was late for a single dose. I used my library card to take out every single book about Helen Keller. Late at night, alone in bed in my room, I would think about her, imagining what it would be like not to be able to see or hear anything. I would close my eyes tightly and cover my ears, finding myself in complete darkness. The fact that Helen Keller, with the love and dedi-cation of her teacher Annie, was able to live a productive life seemed like a miracle to me.

We moved to Sands Point, Long Island, when I was fifteen. The move was traumatic for me—leaving my friends and familiar town behind just as I was starting high school. Our new house was near a facility that was dedicated to Helen Keller. Blind/deaf adults lived there full-time. It seemed like a sign to me, and I immediately signed up to volunteer. I learned how to fingerspell with my hands so that I could communicate with the residents. Every Thursday, I walked over there after school. I was nervous around the residents, but I felt for them and wanted to make their days better. We rode in a van to a local shopping mall, and I helped them with their shopping lists. Toothpaste tubes were opened so the residents could smell and taste the brands. Shampoos were sniffed, foods tasted. They were breaking normal shopping rules, but I understood their need to do so.

On one such outing, I lost track of a resident in a small department store. She was a very thin and nervous girl in her twenties. I walked around the store frantically looking for her, unable to call her by name. When I finally found her, she was spinning inside a big round metal fixture displaying soft women's sweaters. A huge smile filled her face.

"S-s-s-soft!" she yelled when I helped her out by the hand. Her voice was deep and guttural—animallike. I held a sweater up to her cheek, allowing her to feel the softness once more before we went to check out. She laughed out loud, causing me to laugh too. I touched my own face with the material, closing my eyes, imagining how much more she could feel something than I could. With only three out of five senses available, I had learned that taste, smell, and feeling were heightened to levels much more acute than to a person with all five senses intact.

There was another place in Sands Point for children with severe psych issues, including Down syndrome and autism. I quickly signed up to volunteer there too. Some of the children banged their heads against the floor and walls. They picked at their hands and nails until they bled. *These poor little children.* I wanted to help them.

Whenever I traveled outside the facilities with the residents and students, people stared at us. *What are you looking at?* I felt like screaming at them. *Do you think they chose to be like this?* I knew I couldn't fix these people, but I hoped that by spending time with them and treating them kindly and being helpful they would go to sleep at night, having had a better day than they would have had otherwise.

I got a babysitting job with a young boy with Down syndrome. His bedroom was at the top of a steep wooden set of stairs. Inside, there was nothing but a mattress—in great contrast to the beautiful decor in the rest of the family's sprawling, expensive home.

"Why isn't there any other furniture in Danny's room?" I asked his mother the first time I came over.

"If we leave him up there, he'll break things and hurt himself."

There was a lock on the outside his bedroom door.

"Just lock him in if he's bothering you," his parents told me as they left the house. "We do it all the time."

I couldn't believe that Danny's parents were treating him like a wild animal in a cage. I played with him for several hours until his parents got home. There was no way he was going to spend one minute being locked up while I was there.

One evening when I arrived to babysit, Danny wasn't downstairs when his dad let me in. I heard banging and loud yelling coming from upstairs.

"What's going on?"

"Nothing. We just put Danny in his room while we were getting ready to go out," his mom explained.

I hurried up the stairs and unlocked the door. Danny was curled up in the corner, screaming and banging his head against the wall. He looked up at me as I entered the room. His face was covered with streaks of dirty tears, and his hair was matted against his head.

"Hi, Danny!" I went over and sat beside him, smiling at him. His rocking soon slowed, and his cries became whimpers.

"Let's go downstairs and play something. Your mom and dad are gone." He let me hold his hand as we made the trek down the barren stairs.

In high school, I was exposed to my first psychology and sociology classes. Other than writing classes, these were the first teachings that had truly engaged me. "I want to be a psychologist," I told anyone who would listen. "I'm going to get my PhD."

I majored in psychology at William Smith College, and I loved every course I took. While my peers traveled abroad during junior year, I took a full-time internship on a locked ward at a psychiatric hospital. The patients I worked with could not function in the outside world. Most of them had been diagnosed as schizophrenic or psychotic.

This work fascinated me, and Lauren, the clinical director who took me under her wing, taught me as much as she could. I wanted to know more about everything, and she met with me privately almost every day, sharing patient files with me, lending me books, and answering my questions.

"What's the deal with Cathy?" I asked her late Friday morning during the first week of my internship.

"What are you asking?"

"She seems perfectly fine to me. For the first three days, I thought she was staff."

"Read this and then we'll talk." She pulled a file from her desk and handed it to me.

Lauren left me in her office to read the file. As I read Cathy's file, I discovered that she had killed her husband and four young children in cold blood. They had lived in a cabin in the woods, and she had taken a gun and shot up every last one of them. *How is this woman walking around with a smile on her face?* I felt sick to my stomach. Her children had been aged nine, seven, four, and one when she murdered them—two boys and two girls. Cathy's diagnosis was borderline sociopath. *How could somebody kill her children? Didn't she deserve to be dead too?* I steered clear of Cathy from that day on. Even on a locked psych ward, I didn't want to spend too much time with a murderer.

I'm *Not* Stupid After All

Every day during college, I sat in the front of my classes. I was finally one of those students who raised her hand because I knew the answers. I read my works aloud in my creative writing classes, gaining praise from my classmates and professors. I made dean's list every term, graduated Phi Beta Kappa and summa cum laude. And I managed to do all these things while being popular. This was when I first started living a double life—perfect student by day, popular party girl by night.

My college had a mandatory junior year essay that was graded by professors both inside and outside our majors. I wrote my essay during spring break. The break was six weeks long, and I completed my essay in the first five days, freeing myself up for fun and sleep. While my college friends toiled, I was done. I figured it probably sucked but hoped that it would pass.

My essay won first prize. I was shocked. I was granted a two-hundred-dollar check as the prize. I spent the money on cocaine and celebrated with my friends.

I didn't suck at running either. I wasn't that fast, as my brother had pointed out, but I could run far. At the age of thirty-nine, I decided to train for a marathon, and I completed seven over the next ten years. I placed in the top three during many shorter training races. I thought of Jay often, running circles around me and telling me that I wasn't a very good runner. *Jay has never run a marathon,* I would think during my training runs. *I don't suck at running.*

When I was accepted to the University of Pennsylvania for a PhD in counseling psychology, I figured my career path was set. I aced every class the first year, finishing my master's degree in ten months, while doing an internship as a therapist. There was one major problem though. My father was funding my education, and he didn't want me to be a psychologist.

"You're never going to earn a decent living," he said again and again. "Four more years of school after this one and then a dissertation? Your salary will never match the costs. You should go into business." My relationship with my parents had never been great, and this education and career issue was making things increasingly difficult. I knew that I was meant to be helping others, but I was miserable being supported by my dad.

My grandparents left me a small trust that could have paid for the rest of my schooling, but my parents refused to give it to me. Reluctantly, with my dreams shattered, I entered the business world.

For thirty-one years, I worked—eighteen in marketing and then thirteen in real estate. I was successful monetarily, but I was never fulfilled or happy. There were Sunday nights where I actually sobbed, hating the thought that I had to go back to my meaningless job the next day. *I'm making money for big corporations, and all I want to do is help people.* I knew that I would be happier helping even a few people than I was working long hours for corporate America.

During these years, I did what I could to balance meaningless jobs with things that gave me spiritual fulfillment. I volunteered a lot—at soup kitchens feeding the homeless and hungry, at a rehab called the Addiction Institute on the Upper West Side with drug addicts and alcoholics, cofacilitating aftercare programs in the evenings, working at a nonprofit that provided meals for people with terminal illnesses. These were the things that filled my soul and made it possible for me to sell myself out at work in order to pay the bills. *If only I had gotten my PhD,* I thought often. *By now I would be a successful psychologist with a private practice, teaching, doing research, working with people in need of help.*

"They call it work for a reason," my dad told me whenever I complained about my jobs. *Work, not play,* I reasoned with myself. *An end to a means.* Somewhere deep inside me, though, I believed that I could have had both. Meaningful work—that was what I had always wanted. I figured it was too late, and the more time I put into business, the less possible it seemed that I would ever have a truly fulfilling career.

The Men, the Children, the Drugs

In those days, which reached into my early thirties, I married a very conservative guy named Barry and was abstinent from drugs for at least five years. After that breakup, I dated two men back to back who had huge quantities of cocaine on hand. One was my boss, and the other a dealer (who called himself a banker).

Late at night I lay in bed watching the clock move slowly, hating myself: 2:00 a.m., 2:10 a.m., 2:13 a.m. *Why have I done this to myself again?* I would fret. *I have to work tomorrow. I have plans with friends tomorrow. I have to see my parents tomorrow.* Then 3:00 a.m., 4:00 a.m., 5:00 a.m. Still unable to sleep, I hated myself more and more every time I looked at the clock and realized that I was still awake.

Husband number two, Andy, put an end to my cocaine use when our children were babies. With the arrivals of our two-year-old daughter Morgan and Jack, our newborn son, my husband told me that I had to stop. He and I had partied together before my first pregnancy, and my coke use had been minimal between babies and after. I knew he was right, though—I couldn't be a responsible mom and hold down a serious full-time job if I was snorting coke and staying up later than 11:00 p.m. Jack had acid reflux and woke up every two hours for the first year, so I was exhausted enough as it was. I would feed him, and then he would throw up. I would clean him, change him, and put him back in his crib. As soon as I was asleep again, he was awake—crying from hunger. The cycle continued every night. Andy and I were both delirious.

One night when Jack was just a few months old, Andy and I had our date night and we bought some coke. He did a few lines and then went to sleep, while I stayed up the entire night finishing it. Early the next morning Jack began crying, and I was too high to go into his room to help him. Andy came into the living room and saw me sitting there.

"What's wrong with you?" he yelled.

I was terrified—unable to answer him.

He looked at me with disgust and walked into the baby's room.

Andy walked out of Jack's room, holding him in one arm and grabbing a bottle of formula from the refrigerator with the other. "How could you do this?"

I sat mutely, tears of shame rolling from my eyes.

"How are you going to work today? What is wrong with you?"

"I'm sorry!" I cried. *What have I done? I can't even pick my babies up.*

Hours later, after calling his doctor and getting me a Xanax from our nearby pharmacy to calm me down, Andy looked me in the eyes. "If you ever do this again," he promised, "I will take these children away from you." Andy was a criminal defense lawyer, and I believed his threat. Nothing mattered to me more than my precious children. I was petrified.

I stayed dry for thirteen years. "Dry" is the term for addicts who abstain from drugs, but they don't go to 12-step meetings or work a program of recovery. I continued to drink like a lady, which had always been my goal.

Andy and I separated when our children were six and eight. I became a single mom for a few years, liking my freedom most of the time, but feeling overwhelmed by loneliness and self-pity when my children were with their dad. Sometimes I spent holidays alone, wondering why nobody thought to include me in their celebrations. I had always included people who were alone at my events, and I felt sad and resentful when nobody reciprocated.

Within five years I had gotten into a relationship with husband number three. His name was Jordan, and he was pretty conservative and kept me on the straight and narrow. Both of us were trying to manage our adolescent children on our own much of the time, and it was nice to have somebody who understood what it was like. We drank like adults, and both of us were responsible for our children. Drugs were not part of our world. It was comforting to be with a man who was also parenting alone, and we created our own little family unit for about four years—dating for the first two.

My parents were obsessed with Jordan and pushed me to marry him. They hadn't approved of my first two husbands, and I wanted to please them more than anything. They offered to throw us a wedding in Las Vegas, and we agreed. As soon as we were back in Soho, living in my apartment together, I realized that we had made a huge mistake. In retrospect we should have just dated, as combining our families did not work out well, and all of us had been happier apart. My parents were furious when I told them we were breaking up.

"I don't want to meet another man in your life ever again!" my mother said coldly over the telephone.

"Oh, Mallory," my dad said sadly. "You're just never happy. Jordan is such a good man." Once again, I had let my parents down.

The real trouble started when I left Jordan. My children were both teenagers by then. They spent three nights a week with their dad at his apartment. I was free on those nights, and I fell right back into my old habits. I started going out with the kinds of people I had partied with in my twenties and early thirties. These people did coke. I could literally *feel it* when someone was doing coke. If they wiped their nose with their index finger, if their lips moved a certain way, if they were leaving the bar or table more often than was normally necessary. I had a sixth sense when it came to cocaine. I could meet a guy at a bar and *know* that he was high on cocaine, and within an hour we would be buying it together, or holed up in someone's apartment cutting up lines.

Once the cocaine use started again, it got easier and easier for me to find it. I got the number of my old dealer through an old "friend" named Kenneth. These kinds of friends were the druggie friends. They were people that I wouldn't normally hang out with, but since they had the connections that I didn't, I clung on to them tightly. Kenneth's dealer had spent several years in jail during my dry spell, but he was out now. His name was Carl, and he always had the best stuff—pure and uncut. Carl was happy to have me on his "regular" customer list, and the feeling was mutual. Meeting an ex-con on a regular basis didn't even faze me. There was a certain excitement to meeting him on street corners and exchanging cash for drugs.

I had plenty of money now, after working for over twenty-five years and investing well in real estate, and spending a hundred dollars for a gram of coke didn't bother me or impact my lifestyle. In the past, I had been able (sometimes) to buy a gram and save some of it for another time. This was no longer the case. Regardless of my intentions, I never stopped until it was all gone.

If my dealer answers by 1:00 p.m., I'll use today, I would tell myself when I woke up each morning. At 1:00 p.m. I would stretch it. *If he answers by 4:00 p.m., I'll use today. If he calls back by 5:00 p.m., I'll use today.* It was alarming to me when I found myself on the street corner behind my building meeting him at ten one night. I had already been in bed in my pajamas but got up and dressed to meet him nonetheless, when he finally replied after ten hours of my texts and calls.

"Get in," he told me. He was in a Zipcar that night, as he often was. These cars could be rented by the hour rather than by the day, so they were cost-efficient for people who needed them for only a few hours.

"Where were you all day?" I asked once I was inside.

"I was in Brooklyn having dinner."

"I've been calling you since before noon."

"You know I don't turn my phone on until one, baby."

I was pissed, but I couldn't let him know that. I didn't want him to get angry with me, because he could take me off his customer list. I couldn't risk that happening.

"No worries," I said, smiling. "I love you, Carl. See you soon!" I hopped out of the car and put my cutoff straw into the little clear bag, inhaling into one nostril and then the other. The relief was immediate. I knew I would be awake all night until every last drop was gone. I had things to do the next day, but I didn't care.

After a night of using, I would wake up despising myself the next day. *I am not going to use today*, I would promise myself. I could hold off if I stayed home at night, cooking dinner for my children, abstaining from alcohol. But if I went out and ordered a drink, my thumbs would immediately start texting my dealer. An hour later, I would find myself standing outside a local bar or restaurant, waiting for Carl to pull up. The anticipation was always great, and so were the first few snorts.

The problem was always when I got home and locked myself in my bathroom. I did crossword puzzles by hand, or played solitaire and other games on my phone and iPad, smoked cigarettes, snorted little lines for hours. I made it last as long as I could, maintaining that high by myself. My bathroom became my prison. Many nights I was locked inside that room, which was essentially my own little world of addiction. Mark slept down a short hallway to our bedroom in our king-size bed. I tried to stay extremely quiet so he wouldn't wake up and want to come in. I was afraid that he might wake the children, and I couldn't let that happen. I was terrified for them to see me in the state I was in—strung out, afraid to speak, reeking of cigarette smoke. *If I keep doing puzzles, my brain won't atrophy*, I told myself. *Look at me—I just finished the* New York Times' *crossword puzzle. Clearly I'm not destroying my mind.*

Using when I was alone was much easier, but it wasn't feasible once Mark moved in and we got married. He drank a lot, so he usually fell asleep as soon as we got home, but there was always the worry that he would wake up and need to use the bathroom. When this happened, he banged on the door.

"Mallory? Open the door!"

Inside the bathroom, I was gripped with fear. I hid my little stash in the bottom of a metal container that held my cotton balls, closing the mirrored vanity to hide it. "Use another bathroom."

"No! Let me in!" Mark's voice was getting loud, and Morgan's room was right next to ours.

"Quiet," I whispered loudly, cleaning the bathroom up, flushing cigarette butts down the toilet. "You're going to wake the children."

"I don't care! Open the door!"

I was terrified that Morgan and Jack would wake up and see me. I let Mark in to use the bathroom, waited for him to finish so I could lock myself back in again.

"When are you going to sleep?" he asked.

"In fifteen minutes."

Three hours later, I finished my last line and realized that the party was over. This was always the worst part. I struggled to brush my teeth properly, to wash my face, to apply my eye cream and moisturizer. These tasks were essential for me, but flossing was out of the question. If I took a sleeping pill or a downer, I swallowed it and stumbled into bed as quietly as possible. Sometimes the sun was already beginning to lighten the sky outside our bedroom, and I knew Mark's alarm was going to ring momentarily. I would pretend to be asleep so I wouldn't have to speak to him, afraid that my voice would give me away.

This sucks, I told myself time and time again, unable to sleep, or cranky and exhausted the day after. *Why do I keep doing this?* My intentions were always good—to do just a few lines and save the rest for the next night, or for the weekend, or for an upcoming party. But once those first hits entered my body, I was no longer able to stop until I had no more left.

I wanted to tell Mark, but I was afraid that he would leave me. I worried that he would call my dad and my brothers, or tell my children. Several times the words were ready to leave my lips, telling him my dirty secret—but something stopped me. If I told him, I would have to stop, and I wasn't sure I really wanted to.

I was beginning to think the only thing that would stop me would be my own death. The shame that I felt was paralyzing. I had pitied my mother for her drinking, but I was so much worse than her. What kind of a person was I if I couldn't stop doing cocaine? Why couldn't I just stop? Nothing else had ever held me in its grip like this before. I had always been able to achieve the things I really wanted.

At age thirty-eight, I had never run more than four miles, but I decided that I wanted to run the New York City marathon. A year later, I completed my first marathon, crossing the 26.2-mile mark with a smile on my face. By downloading a first timer's training schedule from the New York Road Runners' website, I was able to follow a running and exercise program for four and a half months, achieving a goal that I had never imagined myself capable of. I could control everything else in my life—why couldn't I control my coke habit?

I knew that cocaine was short-term addictive, so thinking that I could stop using it once it was in my possession was insane. The thing I no longer understood was why I kept doing it over and over again. I would promise myself that I was through and then find myself with a straw up my nose again.

On a particularly dark morning after using, I texted Carl: *I have to stop. I'm addicted. My husband says he is going to call the police if I meet you again. He got your number off my phone. Please don't answer my calls or texts.* This was all untrue, of course, as Mark had no idea that I had a dealer or that I was doing coke.

Carl did not text back.

Three days later I was out having dinner and drinks with friends. I was exhausted and really wanted to do some coke. I texted Carl: *Hey. Greenwich and Desbrosses?* No reply. I went outside and called him, and my call was cut short after one ring. Carl must have blocked me. I sent a text to my "friend" Kenneth, who had introduced me to Carl. *Hey. What are you up to? Want to meet?*

I'm at home with the baby.

Can you call Carl for me? He won't answer my calls or texts.

Why not?

Long story.

I can't tonight. My wife will kill me. I was out last night.

What had I done? Now my prime source wouldn't answer my calls or texts. I should never have told him to cut me off.

I sent Carl another text the next day. He still wouldn't answer. I called him at 1:00 p.m., and he answered.

"Hey, Carl, I'm really sorry about that text I sent you the other day. I made the whole thing up. Can you meet me?"

"You have to come here. My guy George will meet you. And don't send those texts again," he warned me.

I had sent them in the past, and sometimes Carl wouldn't speak to me for a week or longer. I was able to buy from other people who worked and hung out in my neighborhood haunts sometimes, but it usually took a lot more time and effort. I jumped into a cab to meet his guy, who was a skinny, young dude with short blond dreadlocks. He appeared from nowhere, slinking down the East Village block where we always met, looking like any other NYU student coming out of his sublet to buy a pack of cigarettes or a Red Bull.

"Great to see you!" I told him, kissing him on both cheeks.

"What are you up to today?" he asked.

I thought it was strange that he even cared, but maybe he was just being polite. "Nothing much. Just hanging with my son."

It was actually true. I would go home, do some lines at my desk before Jack got home, and then play solitaire on my computer. Jack would come home after school, say hello, eat a snack, and go into his room and play games on his computer, or do some homework. I could see him sitting at his desk through the windows in our rooms—our apartment was built around a big outdoor courtyard, and my window gave me a perfect view of his back. When I saw him get up from his desk chair, I hid my coke and straw in my pocket. I knew I had to feed him dinner, but the later it got, the less motivated I became to cook him something. The cocaine took my appetite away, and sometimes I hoped he would forget that he was supposed to eat.

"Hey, Mom," he would eventually call out as he entered my room. "What's for dinner?"

"Coming! Want to help me make some stir-fried chicken with vegetables and rice?"

"Sure," he'd say happily. "I'm starving."

We would cook side by side, and then I'd push a small plate of the delicious meal around with my fork, trying to get a few bites down. Jack loved my cooking, and it made me happy to watch him eating seconds. As soon as he finished, and his dishes were done, we would each retreat back to our own rooms.

One night I stayed up particularly late, locked in the bathroom. Jack had stayed at his dad's apartment the night before, and Morgan had just started college in Upstate New York. The only pills that I had to help me sleep were Trazodone, which is an antidepressant often prescribed as a nonaddictive sleeping pill. I was prescribed one fifty milligram pill a night. That night I took three, because I didn't think one would do the job.

I woke up on the stone floor of my bathroom. *I must have fallen asleep*, I thought. *I'd better get into bed before Mark finds me in here.* Placing my hands on the counter, I pulled myself up.

I woke up on the floor again. *How did that happen? I must have fainted.* Again, I pulled myself up to standing.

"Mal?" I heard. I was on the floor again. My head hurt.

"Mallory, are you okay?" Mark called out from the bedroom.

Was I okay? I wasn't sure. I stood up. Our large stainless steel and glass bathroom scale was broken on the floor. My head must have hit it when I fell down the third time.

"I fell down," I answered. "I broke the scale."

Mark tried to come in, but the door was locked. I crawled over and unlocked it.

"I'm dizzy. Can you help me?"

Mark grabbed on to my arm and helped me to bed. I sat up against the pillows, my legs spread out.

"What happened?" Mark asked, standing over me. My head was spinning. I sat up. My head was killing me.

"My head hurts." I touched the back of my head, and it was wet. My fingers were covered with blood. "I'm bleeding." There was a bump on the left side of my head. It was the size of a softball, and it was throbbing.

"Do you want to go to the hospital?"

"No!" I was terrified they would find drugs in my system if I went to the hospital.

My head was killing me. I couldn't get comfortable in any position. Sitting, standing, and lying down were all making me dizzy. I probably had a concussion. The bump was still bleeding. Mark got me an ice pack, which I tried to apply. The pain was terrible, and the cold pressure from the frozen ice pack was making it worse.

Mark started getting ready to go to the gym downstairs in our condo building to work out with our trainer. Our regular weekday time was 6:30 a.m. There were many mornings when I dragged myself down there after a night of partying. *I'm either going to sweat the toxins out or I'm going to die*, I would tell myself. I knew that a stroke or heart attack were both possible.

"Mark, I need to talk to you."

"Okay," he called out from his closet.

"Please come here," I heard myself saying. "I need your complete attention." I patted the bed next to where I was sitting. He sat down, and I looked at him. I was finally going to tell him the truth—I had to. I was dying, and I couldn't stop myself from doing cocaine.

"I fell down because I was doing drugs," I told him as I looked at his handsome face, his beautiful green eyes protected by his expensive designer glasses.

"What drugs?" Mark asked. "Ambien?"

"No. I stopped doing Ambien when I hurt myself before. I've been doing coke, and I can't stop."

"Do you want to go to rehab?" he asked me, looking sad and concerned.

"I can't go to rehab! I have to stop on my own. I don't want anybody else to know. Promise me you won't tell anyone."

Mark looked so sad. "I promise."

Nobody can know that I'm a coke addict. Everyone will judge me and think I'm pathetic. I need to do this myself.

"I have to go down to the gym," he told me. "I'm going to be late."

He walked out of our bedroom, and I heard the front door open and then close behind him. I sat on our bed, crying. I wished that Mark had stayed in our bedroom, holding and comforting me. I wished that he could fix me, but I knew that he couldn't. Mark didn't like to address problems—he was much more comfortable putting on a good face. His whole family was the same way. *At least he isn't divorcing me. Not yet anyway.*

The pain from my head was unbearable, so I couldn't even lie down comfortably. I felt like I was on a roller coaster, a Ferris wheel, and a merry-go-round all at once. The dizziness and spinning continued—I was in terrible pain. I knew that I could have died if my head had hit something sharper or harder. I was lucky to be alive, but it didn't feel that way.

I cried some more. I didn't know what else to do.

Look at Me, I've Turned into My Mother

My mother never liked eating, probably because food got in the way of her alcohol intake. Before dinner, on an average day, she drank black coffee with Sweet'n Low and sipped clear chicken consommé that her housekeeper carried to her on a bed tray. At night when she was forced to join my father for dinner, there was a lot of fighting.

"Goddamn it, Lillian," my father would say, "would you eat something, please?"

"I am eating," she'd say, pushing the food around on her plate. She always had a cigarette going at the dinner table in those days, before smoking became taboo. Her long Benson and Hedges 100s smoldered in the cluttered ashtray while she guzzled her drink.

She tried to get rid of her food like a bad child, offering it to everyone else at the table. My mother always complained that her dish had more food on it than everyone else's. She tried to trade plates with my brothers and me. She placed big pieces of her meal on other people's plates, and then, looking miserable, moved what was left on her own plate around with a fork and a knife.

"Pass me that wine, honey, would you?" my mother asked whoever was closest to it. "My last glass was so little."

There was not a drink she didn't like. Waiters could bring after-dinner drinks to a table of eight, and seven of us sipped at ours to be polite and then pushed them away. My mother downed hers and then quietly consumed as many of the remaining seven as possible before my father noticed what she was doing and exploded.

"Goddamn it, Lillian! That's enough!" He looked both sad and angry at the same time. The deep lines in his forehead wrinkled up, and sweat beads formed at his hairline. She ignored him, continuing to down as much alcohol as possible before it was taken away.

The story never changed. Night after night, my mother drank and my father yelled. My mother drank some more and didn't eat. My father yelled. My father poured more alcohol into her glass, and she drank it. My father yelled some more. My mother continued to drink, ignoring him completely.

It was exhausting to watch. After dinner, my father would go into their bedroom and get ready for bed. He was an early riser and needed his sleep. While he was smoking cigarettes in his bedroom and watching television, my mother sat in the kitchen by herself, smoking too. She called people on the phone and tried to engage them in conversation while my father slept.

Sometimes she passed out on the kitchen chair, and my little brother or I would move her onto the floor, placing a pillow under her head and covering her with a blanket. She was deadweight—too heavy to move any farther. In the morning, she would be gone by the time we woke up, and nobody mentioned the night before.

My mother drove drunk and crashed cars all the time. Once she drove her car right into the back of my father's car in our driveway. She hit trees on the side of our road and crashed into the stone pillars on our driveway. One time she drove her car right through our garage into our newly renovated playroom.

She was truly a mess. She would fall onto sidewalks and down steps outside restaurants. She often had trouble getting in and out of the car to get home. Usually she landed on her head and woke up with big bumps on her forehead—her skin black and blue. She took to wearing colorful scarves around her head for months on end, covering the bruises and dents. Large hematomas covered her legs. Going to the doctor was not an option for her—she deplored doctors. (God forbid one of them would figure out what was going on.)

Having friends sleep over was a nightmare. I was always afraid that they would want to go into the kitchen for a late-night snack and find her clad in a see-through nightgown, drunkenly waving her cigarette around while she talked on the phone. Or worse, she might venture down to my room to visit us, holding her left hand out in front of her as a make-shift ashtray as her cigarette ashes grew longer in her right hand.

Her body was not one that anyone wanted to look at naked, and having her flaunt it was horrifying for me and my brothers. She had been a beautiful young woman, but by age forty, the alcohol made her breasts and stomach sag. Her long, thin legs had been her best asset, but they were now unshaven, the skin flaky and dry. Her beautiful face lost most of its allure by the time she was forty—her sculpted cheekbones were hollow, and her dark striking eyes were now dull and puffy. Her once-long wavy brown hair now hung limply, dandruff falling all over everything. Her favorite color was black, so all her tops were stained with ashes and flakes.

I pitied my mother. She had been rich, beautiful, and glamorous in her younger years, before her drinking took over. Pictures of her in her teens and twenties showed movie-star beauty, and as a young child, I remember her heading out for the evening, leaving a trail of sequins behind her, mink or sable jackets covering her gowns.

Drinking robbed her of her friends, her good humor, and her ability to show up as a supportive and loving mother. I craved her acceptance and her company, but the good moments were always cut short, and the absences left a much-greater mark than the brief and drunken promises of a better tomorrow, which were always forgotten in the shadow of the morning hangover. A specially planned shopping spree for us turned into a snobby lunch of tea sandwiches at Lord & Taylor's restaurant, followed by a stomachache, which eliminated the shopping as she had to rush home to use her own toilet.

"I want to look at Wayne Rogers shirts," I told her once on the way to Lord & Taylor. "I love them so much!" Many of my friends now owned these expensive and highly coveted button-downs, and I was hoping that my mother would buy me one.

"Oh, my god," she said as she paid the restaurant bill. "I'm about to have terrible diarrhea. We have to get home."

"Why can't you use the bathroom here?"

"I can only 'make' in my own toilet."

I was so disappointed, but I knew from experience that our shopping spree had ended before it ever began. Each time we planned some time together, I was hopeful that we would finally have some real mother-daughter bonding, but it never ended up that way. We always drove home in silence.

While I was touring colleges, she canceled visits last minute because she was unable to rouse herself from bed after a particularly toxic evening of precelebration. In pure alcoholic style, she sabotaged everything good that she ever promised me. The night of the rehearsal dinner for my first wedding, she was unable to make it, leaving old friends and relatives from out of town bewildered with her absence.

My mother died shortly after her seventy-third birthday. I was forty-eight years old. She was mostly bedridden by that time, addled with COPD and alcoholism. Her portable oxygen tank had taken over several years earlier as her must-have accessory. Some days she rallied, but mostly she was at home, alone in bed. My father prepared beautiful little meals for her, trying to entice her to eat as if she were a finicky child. The night she died, my father made her a bowl of ice cream before she went to sleep; it was Breyer's chocolate mixed with black cherry. She ate every bite. He was so happy that she had eaten as her appetite had been minimal for months. She told him she loved him, went to sleep, and never woke up.

Imagine my horror just two years after my mother died when I looked into my bathroom mirror one morning and saw her looking back at me. I had a black eye and a fat lip. My cheekbone was broken, and the right side of my face was blown up like a water balloon. A hematoma ran from my waist on the right side down to my knee.

I woke up with an ice pack on my face and another on my right hip. I vaguely remembered taking them out of the freezer in the early morning hours after my precious dachshund woke me, needing to go outside. I had slipped and fallen into the radiator, smashing my face and the right side of my body. I knew I was hurt, but the hours of alcohol, cocaine, and Ambien had me so wasted that I was lucky to make it back into bed alive. When I walked into the bathroom and saw myself, my blood ran cold through my veins. I had a school event to attend for my son Jack the next day. I had work appointments scheduled. I showered and dressed quickly and cabbed over to my dermatologist's office in Tribeca.

"Oh, Mallory!" he exclaimed. He was so beautiful and gay and brilliant—I adored him. "What have you gone and done now?"

Before I could answer, he continued, "Don't tell me…it was Ambien, wasn't it?"

"Yes," I admitted, omitting the alcohol and cocaine. "How did you know?"

"The craziest things happen to my patients when they take Ambien!" he said. "One guy called and texted me all night, and the next day he apologized, saying he had taken Ambien. Throw that stuff out, girlfriend! It will kill you."

"I will," I promised him. "But why is my face so puffy and crackly?" I demonstrated how, if I pushed on the puffiness, it made a squishing sound as if it were filled with liquid bubbles.

"Don't push that in," he warned me. "Your cheekbone is probably broken. The liquid from your sinuses is leaking through. You don't want to get an infection."

Even this didn't stop me. I took pictures of my awful-looking face and body and looked at them for several weeks whenever I wanted to get high. Instead of reminding me of why I shouldn't call my dealer, the pictures depressed me so much that I wanted to numb my shameful feelings more than ever. Eventually I deleted the pictures, no longer wanting the reminder.

I was so riddled with shame and guilt that I truly wanted to die.

"Mark," I told my husband one night, not long after that fall, "when I die, I want to be cremated."

"Okay," he said.

"I don't like the idea of being buried," I continued. "I don't want bugs eating me, or cold rain falling on me. I want my children to get some of my ashes, and the rest should be strewn on the beach in Delray on a warm, sunny day."

Mark did not like these kinds of conversations. He didn't like to discuss illness or death.

"And I don't want an autopsy to be performed on me. I don't want to be all cut up. Just cremated, please."

Mark's eyes were already glazed over with disinterest. I realized that I would need to make these changes to my will immediately, and I did that same week. I didn't think that my husband's brain would even retain this conversation once I was dead, so I had to cover my bases.

I figured that I would die from a stroke or a heart attack or from another fall. I really didn't care as long as my secret was never revealed. My children would get my money and my apartment, so they would be fine. I loved them more than life itself, but not enough to stop me from chasing the high that I could no longer stop. As long as nobody knew that I was weak like my mother had been, and her mother before her, it would be okay. I would die quickly like both of them had, but I had hidden my addiction where they hadn't. Nobody would judge me in death because nobody knew my terrible secret.

Recovery

Please Help Me

I sat in temple on the Upper West Side between my husband and my father-in-law. It was the Holy Holidays, or I wouldn't have been there. I wasn't religious, though I did like being Jewish. The only reason that I went to temple at all was because it made my husband and his parents happy, and I liked pleasing them.

I was in a very bad place inside. I was hiding my drug addiction from everyone close to me, and I couldn't stop. I had tried so many different ways, and nothing was working. A very expensive addiction psychiatrist on the Upper East Side tried to hypnotize me into stopping. She had taped a penny onto the wall in her office.

"Now focus on the penny," she directed me.

At three-hundred and seventy-five dollars for a forty-five-minute session, I was focusing very hard. This psychiatrist seemed like a joke to me since I started meeting with her, but she was happy to prescribe me Ambien, Xanax, and Trazodone, so I kept seeing her. I learned that I needed pills to get me down when my coke supply ran out, and my dealer charged a fortune if I bought them from him. A downtown psychiatrist that I had worked with previously had fired me because I wasn't willing to stop drinking and drugging, and this was where I ended up—staring at a penny on an ecru wall, having no belief that hypnosis would work.

I had gone to all kinds of medical doctors, hoping that someone would find something very wrong with me so I would be hospitalized and unable to continue doing coke. None of them had found anything wrong. I knew I was going to die, but I couldn't stop.

The rabbi was speaking, and I was barely listening, caught up in my own nightmare. He was the very same rabbi who had married Mark and me in his chambers upstairs only a year earlier. But then I heard him say, "Take a moment of silent prayer." I closed my eyes and said silently, *Please help me.*

I didn't believe in God, but I figured it couldn't hurt to ask for help. *Please help me,* I prayed again the next day when the rabbi directed us to pray. *Please help me.* We were surrounded by stained glass, soaring ceilings, and other worshippers, many dressed in their newest fall outfits, but all I noticed was the rabbi. All I heard was the rabbi saying, "Take a moment of silent prayer."

I hadn't prayed regularly since I was a young child, reciting my evening vows. If and when I did pray, it was always for something specific, or to get me out of trouble.

A few weeks later, I found myself waiting in the office of a new doctor. I made these appointments frequently—surely some doctor would realize that I had a drug problem and help me. If not that, someone was sure to find a brain tumor or something equally serious—something that would cause me to stop drugging.

I found this doctor on the internet. I liked him for two reasons: his office was in Soho, on the same street that I lived on, and he was both an MD and a PhD in psychology. *He must be empathetic if he's a psychologist,* I thought when I read his credentials online.

I began filling out paperwork, and I didn't really like the office. The waiting room was very small, and the furniture was pretty shabby. I didn't like the way the other patients looked either. The files on open shelves behind the receptionist looked unprofessional.

I texted my husband: *I don't like this doctor's office.*

Why?

Seems dirty and unprofessional.

So leave.

Mark was used to this. I was always texting him from different doctors' offices, asking his permission to bail before I even spoke to them.

I was about to tell the receptionist that I was leaving when the doctor walked right up to me, his body shading my iPhone. "Mallory Neuberger?" he asked.

"Yes," I answered, following his short self into a tiny examining room.

"What's up?" he asked me. His kind brown eyes looked into mine. I knew he was Jewish from his name and the fact that he had studied in Israel, and he looked and sounded gay. I felt immediately safe and comfortable.

"I'm living a double life," I told him, surprising myself with these words, and with the tears welling up in my eyes. "I eat healthy and run marathons. I'm a mom and a wife, and I have a good job. I'm doing coke and drinking and smoking and taking sleeping pills. I keep falling on my head."

"You're going to fucking die," he told me. "Go to Hazelden on Twenty-Sixth Street and Eighth Avenue. They have an IOP."

"What's that?"

"Intensive outpatient treatment. They meet several times a week for a few hours each time."

I couldn't believe it. He had used the f-word, and there was actually an outpatient program right in Manhattan, just a short ride from my apartment! Why didn't I know that?

I left his office with Hazelden's number in my hand. I didn't even go home but called them from the sidewalk. They told me to come right over for an intake interview. On the way I called Mark and told him my good news—I could go to treatment without leaving home.

My interviewer was amazing. He was a coke addict who was in recovery, and I told him my story, crying for the second time that morning. He cried along with me. It was a Thursday, and he told me that my case would be presented to the board the next day, and if I were accepted, I would begin on Monday. I couldn't believe that I could get help on Mondays through Thursdays from 1:30 p.m. to 4:30 p.m. right near my home. My son and daughter wouldn't need to know. I didn't have to go away for help, so nobody would need to know. I was so relieved but also petrified that Hazelden might not find me fit for their program.

"There's a C.A. meeting right near here," the intake guy told me. "You should go. It starts at twelve thirty."

"What's C.A.?" I asked him.

"Cocaine Anonymous."

I had no idea there was a program called Cocaine Anonymous. I was thrilled. Coke had always been my problem. I was terrified of what the other people at the meeting would be like, but I walked the few short blocks over and rang the buzzer that was marked "C.A." I couldn't believe that people admitted they were going to C.A. meetings, and I was very worried that someone on the street or coming in or out of the building would see where I was going. I was desperate though, so I spoke into the buzzer when a man called out "C.A.! How can I help you?"

"I'm here for the meeting," I answered.

The buzzer rang, and the voice said, "Ninth floor."

I took the elevator up and found a room marked "C.A. Office." I went inside where three people were sitting in a stark, windowed room. There were all kinds of signs on the walls:

Easy Does It

Progress Not Perfection

One Day at a Time

There were signs with 12-Steps and 12-Traditions. I had no idea what any of this was. However, when the first man introduced himself as "Al, Crackhead and Alcoholic," I breathed a sigh of relief. When they came to me, I said, "I'm Mallory. I'm a cocaine addict."

"Hi, Mallory!" the other three people called out cheerfully. "Welcome!"

I cried for the third time that day, sharing the horrors of my inability to stop doing cocaine once I had started. I told them how I couldn't sleep and would lie awake for hours, watching the minutes tick by on the clock, knowing I had places to be and things to do, but not being able to stop myself.

"I lost my two children due to my addiction," the one other woman shared, tears running down her face. She was from Utah, visiting Manhattan for only one day with her coke addict husband who was at the meeting with her. Her name was Mandy, and she looked like an innocent woman. I couldn't imagine her doing drugs. She was clean-cut and preppy. "Today I'm married, and I have my children back. I'm working on my master's degree to be an addiction counselor." She was clean for nine years, her husband for six. They had met at an A.A. meeting in Utah and started their own branch of C.A. there.

Al had been a mean drunk and a crack addict. He was seven years sober and seemed peaceful and happy. At the end of the meeting, we stood in a mini circle with our arms around each other.

"God, grant me the serenity to accept the things I cannot change," they said in unison. "The courage to change the things I can, and the wisdom to know the difference. Keep coming back! It works if you work it, so work it, you're worth it, and live it!"

I had no idea what they were talking about, but they were all sober from the one thing I couldn't control. I needed to be around these people. Al and Mandy took my phone numbers and gave me theirs.

I was completely wiped out from my morning, from all my honesty and tears. I took my phone out on the sidewalk and texted my dealer.

You around?

Fourteenth and Third, he texted back immediately.

It was meant to be, I told myself, hailing a cab.

"Fourteenth and Third," I told the driver.

When Mark got home that night, he found me sitting at my desk snorting cocaine and playing solitaire.

"What are you doing?" he asked. He had never seen me do coke before.

"Hazelden told me to do as much coke as I want until Monday to get it out of my system."

"Okay," he said, turning on the news.

Al sent me a text the next morning at around eleven: *How are you?*

I was exhausted from lack of sleep and feeling completely depressed that I had used again the night before.

Terrible. I went to my dealer right after the meeting and used again. Come to the meeting today at 12:30.

I poured myself another cup of coffee and jumped into the shower. Al hugged me when I walked into the meeting.

"Don't beat yourself up," he told me, looking at me with his smiling green eyes, holding on to my elbows with his hands. We were about the same height with my three-inch platforms on, and he looked right into me. "It's okay," he promised me, "you're here now."

I started my IOP at Hazelden three days later—much to my relief. While I was filling out my paperwork, I noticed a line that stated no alcohol could be consumed during the course of treatment.

"I can't sign this," I told the young administrative woman who was sitting with me. "I'm not here to stop drinking. I'm just here to stop doing coke."

"This is a total abstinence program," she told me, looking a little uncomfortable.

"I can't stop drinking," I insisted. "I'm not going to be able to come here."

She asked me to wait and left the small office. When she came back, she was with another woman, this one older and more professional looking. Her badge confirmed her importance: "Karen Lane, clinical director."

"Hi, Mallory," Karen began, looking at the papers in front of me. "What seems to be the problem?"

"I'm not an alcoholic," I told her. "I just need to stop doing coke. I can't stop drinking. My entire life is about drinking."

She read the passage that I was pointing to.

"I see," she said, looking thoughtful. "How about if we change the language to say that you will try not to drink during the course of your treatment?"

"You can change it, but I'm not going to stop drinking."

She changed the language, and I initialed the passage. This was bullshit—there was no way I could live without alcohol. Alcohol was legal. I loved drinking. My husband and I were drinking buddies. We met drinking and had been drinking together for the last four years. All our friends drank. All we did was drink, every night. We went to wine tastings and fancy wine dinners at restaurants. We had dinner parties with our friends, piling up the corks on the counters like victory badges. In fact, my cocaine use had enabled me to drink more than ever before, turning me from a lightweight drinker into a woman with a pretty good tolerance. Without coke, I was ready for bed after two glasses of wine, but with it, I could stay up all night. A couple of hits every half hour or so, and I was as good as new—a fun party girl.

In my first process group on that Monday, I was asked by the therapist to introduce myself.

"I'm Mallory, and I'm a cocaine addict," I told the men and women sitting around the circle of ten with me. "I'm not an alcoholic," I continued, "and I am going to drink tonight, even though Hazelden says I should try not to drink during the course of treatment." I expected to see nodding heads, but instead I noticed a few people diverting their gazes from me, maybe even looking pissed off.

I went out in my neighborhood that night, happy with my new coke-free lifestyle. I hadn't done cocaine since Thursday, so today was day 3 without it. I was with two friends, and I ordered a glass of wine. Before I finished half the glass, I was craving cocaine in every inch of my body.

I put my phone in my lap and texted my dealer: *You around? Spring and Washington?*

No answer.

I went into the bathroom and called him. The call went right to voice mail.

"Let's go somewhere else," I said to my friends when it was clear that my dealer was not responding to me. "This place sucks tonight."

Two bars later, I was still coming up dry. None of my usual sources had anything for me. Normally the bartenders and owners of my neighborhood favorites could hook me up, or there were a few neighbors who hung out regularly who had connections too.

It was getting late, and I had IOP the next day. I called it a night with my friends and walked across the street to my apartment building. The terrible cravings had finally passed. As I walked by the doorman's desk, my phone rang—it was my dealer! I hit Decline. I turned my phone off, went into my apartment, and locked the door.

I have not had a drink since.

I Wish I Was Sober, You Wish You Were Drunk

Geri and I became fast friends in our late twenties. We met through a mutual friend and quickly bonded over cocaine and white wine dinners. We both liked to shoot pool, and we were amateur hustlers—an attractive blonde (her) and brunette (me), sinking angle shots like nobody's business.

We hung out in my bachelorette pad at One Astor Place, doing lines and drinking wine, and then we'd walk over to Café Tabac for a late dinner. My brown miniature poodle was our favored accessory, and he would sit on a banquette between us, eating french fries and sipping water out of our glasses.

"Chardonnay, please!" we would call out as we entered. It was the place to be seen back then, and we loved it. Light French fare, which we never touched, unending glasses of wine, and our frequent visits to the ladies' room to freshen up our nostrils.

"We're almost out," Geri told me one night.

"Let's go get some more." The night was young, and so were we.

We drove uptown in her husband's new sports car. I was behind the wheel, because Geri wasn't comfortable driving stick. We sped up the FDR highway, eager to reach our destination. I was going seventy miles an hour.

"I wonder what the speed limit is up here," I asked.

"Probably sixty-five," she said. *Probably not,* but we didn't care.

Geri was a pretty woman, always sporting a ponytail and a pair of jeans and cowboy boots. The more wasted we got, the more she complained—about her husband, her apartment, not having as much money as she wanted. She repeated herself over and over, her words beginning to slur. To me she seemed to have everything she needed, but she was a girl who always wanted more.

Geri's husband Michael despised me. He was a control freak, and Geri was the person he tried to control the most. He was handsome and successful, and Geri was not willing to be told what to do, especially by him. He didn't want his wife snorting cocaine, but when we were together, he knew that it was inevitable. He sat quietly and watched us, drinking his scotch and chain-smoking Marlboro Reds.

"Come on, Geri," he urged her. "We should get home."

"Don't be a party pooper!" Geri told him. "We're just getting started here."

One night when we double-dated, Geri complimented my date on his shirt.

"I like yours too," my date said, looking at her white T-shirt. "Wanna trade?"

"Sure," Geri said quickly, pulling her shirt over her head. We were at Raoul's, another one of our drinking holes. Michael looked at his wife, sitting at our booth in her lacy bra. Michael just shook his head, looking sad as the shirt swap commenced.

Eventually, Michael bought a house in Kings Point and moved Geri away from me. It was only a thirty-minute drive, but we rarely saw each other once they moved, and they started a family. We spoke on the phone occasionally, and Geri had found some people who did coke near her. She was partying with them and drinking a lot.

"I'm sorry I haven't seen you, Mal," she said sadly. "But I've been a real mess. I can't even take care of the baby."

She was drinking every day, often starting as early as noon. When she finished an open bottle of wine in her refrigerator, she drove to the liquor store to buy another bottle so Michael wouldn't notice. She would drink that bottle down to the same level as the first one.

"I hit a car in the liquor store parking lot last week," she told me. "So now I have my housekeeper driving me there." Geri was falling asleep before seven every night, leaving Michael to care for their baby son.

The years passed, and we were both busy having babies and careers. At one point, I didn't hear from Geri again for almost a year.

"Mal," Geri said one day when I answered the phone, "I have a big favor to ask you."

"What?"

"I'm celebrating a year sober," she told me. "I really want you to come to my anniversary at my A.A. meeting."

What? Geri was sober? When had this happened?

Geri gave me the details, and I drove out to Great Neck and arrived at the church where she told me the celebration would be taking place. Geri was sitting at the front table, and she looked amazing. She seemed more relaxed than I had ever seen her.

"Hi, I'm Geri. I'm a drug addict and an alcoholic."

"Hi, Geri!" the room responded.

I looked around the room. Everybody looked so happy. I noticed Geri's parents and her sister sitting along the wall. *How could she say she's a drug addict in front of her family?*

Geri told her story, and I was very moved. She spoke of the misery of her addiction to coke and alcohol and how she could not stop until she started going to A.A. meetings. She thanked her sponsor and her family. She was presented with a one-year medallion. I drove home thinking that I had lost a friend. I couldn't believe that her addiction had gotten so bad that she had told her family and gotten sober. Michael looked so smug at the meeting that I wasn't able to meet his eyes.

I went on to drink for another ten years and snorted coke for the last few. The few times I saw Geri she had arrived at my parties with her sponsor, carrying packets of gum and sucking candies, always clutching a bottle of diet soda. When I was coming up on ninety days sober, I was asked to speak at a C.A. meeting one night. I called Geri and asked her to come. She and Michael arrived into the packed room a few minutes late, and I was already telling my story of brokenness and unmanageability. Her smile was gigantic, and she waved to me across the room.

"I'm so proud of you," she mouthed.

When I finished speaking, Geri's hand shot up. "I'm Geri, and I'm a drug addict and an alcoholic." Geri had recently celebrated ten years without a drink or a drug. At ninety days sober, ten years seemed like an eternity, something I couldn't even fathom.

"Hi, Geri!" everyone replied.

"Mallory and I go a long way back," she started. "She was my running buddy. We were out of control, but we had a lot of fun back then. I have to admit, when Mallory called me and told me she was celebrating ninety days, I was kind of jealous." I was confused, and a lot of other people looked surprised too. "I just celebrated ten years clean and sober, and when Mallory told me she was just getting clean, I wished that I had been out there with her for those ten years."

I was shocked at her words.

"Believe me," I told her on the phone the next day, "you weren't missing anything. I was miserable the last few years. If anyone should be jealous, it's me."

This is the nature of our disease. In recovery we can still romanticize drinking and taking drugs. Whenever someone relapses and then comes back into the program, I ask them how it was *out there.* One guy from the 7:00 a.m. meeting at Crossroads answered me perfectly.

"It was great for about thirty minutes, and those were the thirty minutes between when I called my dealer and when he showed up."

I haven't heard a single person say that their relapse was fun or worth it. And sometimes they never come back. There are so many people I met at meetings who went out and I have never heard from again, even women I have sponsored, who were desperate to remain sober while I worked with them—until they weren't. I pray that they are all alive and well.

Ten days after I got sober, Hurricane Sandy hit Manhattan. I had started my IOP at Hazelden and was going to meetings every day. Downtown New York City was without power, and after a few nights living in the darkness in our Soho loft, Mark, Jack, and I were able to get a hotel room that accepted dogs on the Upper West Side. Hazelden was shut down and not answering their phones, and I felt like a ship without water. I went to meetings every day while Jack and Mark wandered around the Upper West Side. Walking back from my meeting one day, I called my father.

"Hi, honey," he answered, "how are you doing there?"

"I'm in rehab, Dad."

"Oh, my god!" he said. "Where are you?"

"Well, I'm in New York, and my rehab at Hazelden is closed right now, but I'm almost two weeks sober. I'm in a program from Monday to Thursday every week, between one and four o'clock."

"You poor thing," he said. I thought I heard tears in his voice. *He probably thinks I got it from my mom and he feels badly.*

"I'm getting sober from drugs," I admitted.

"Oh, no," he said. "I had no idea." His voice was so kind and forgiving, tears started falling down my cheeks. "What drugs were you taking?"

"I'm a cocaine addict," I told him. These were the words I had held inside for years, fearing that my father, my brothers, my husband, my children, my friends would never speak to me again.

I remembered hearing Geri say that she was a drug addict and an alcoholic nine years earlier, in front of her parents and sister. Then I didn't believe I would ever be able to say those words aloud.

"I can't drink either," I told my dad. "That's the worst part. I didn't think I was an alcoholic, but Hazelden told me that I'm cross-addicted, so I can't take anything mood or mind-altering."

"You're a strong lady," my dad told me. "Remember when your mom got sober for a little while?"

"I do remember." She never seemed happier to me, but she didn't stick with it.

"Keep in touch, okay?" my dad said. "Let me know how you're doing."

"I will," I promised.

As soon as we hung up, I decided to call my brothers and tell them too. *The more people I tell, the more account-able I'll be,* I figured. Nobody in my family has abandoned me because I don't drink or do drugs any more. Some of my friends are no longer really friends, but that's okay. If my sobriety is unacceptable to people, then I have to respect that and stay away. They know I'm in recovery though, and if they ever need help or know someone else who does, I'm here waiting to extend my hand.

I Can't Keep You Sober, I Can't Make You Drink

I had two sponsors during my first year of recovery. A sponsor is someone who guides you through the 12-steps by sharing their experience, strength, and hope with you. My first sponsor was a gay man named Rick, and we worked the first eight steps together before having a difference of opinion, which led to a breakup. Rick flipped out on me on the phone one night when I mentioned that I took Lexapro and wanted to decrease my dosage.

"Mallory," he said, clearly agitated, "why didn't you tell me that you take medication?"

In recovery, it was understood that we could not take any mood- or mind-altering substances, regardless of our particular addiction. For example, a coke addict could not drink or smoke weed, and an alcoholic couldn't take Xanax, even if it was prescribed. Lexapro was not mood or mind-altering.

Why would I tell you? You're not a doctor.

"You never asked me," I explained. "Why would you care? It's an antianxiety medication that I've taken for years."

"This isn't good. You're compartmentalizing your recovery." He sounded angry, and judgmental, which really wasn't like him.

What was he talking about? I told the man everything about my life—every day.

"Rick, why would I mention that I take Lexapro? You're not my doctor or my therapist. I discuss that with them. Now, when are you free to get together this week to start working on my ninth step? I want to start making my amends."

The ninth step was making amends to people we had harmed, as long as we didn't harm them or others by doing so. I had a long list, and I wanted to clean things up with people I had hurt.

I was anxious to finish my steps by my first year anniversary so I could begin to sponsor other women. In New York, the general rule was that you could sponsor when you had achieved these two things.

"I want to get together and talk about the fact that you're not telling me everything first," he said, sounding more like a teacher than a sponsor. "I think we need to slow down on your steps for a bit."

I was pissed. I really wanted to keep moving on my steps, and one step a month was my goal. This was going to screw up my plan. But I knew that I had to meet with him in person to discuss it, or he wouldn't continue working the steps with me. So later that week, I rode my bicycle up to Chelsea to meet him. My mind was made up—I wasn't going to work with him anymore. Who was he to judge me and care about a prescription medication that I took for my anxiety and moodiness. Lexapro had kept my moods more even for a very long time. I had a psychiatrist for this, an expert who was trained in such things.

"There are too many people involved in your recovery, Mallory," he began when we sat down together in the C.A. office where we had met eight months earlier. "I feel that you're telling some things to your therapist, some to your doctor, some to your counselor at Hazelden, and some to me. As your sponsor, I need to know everything."

"Rick, I think it's time that I find a new sponsor. I want to finish my steps in the next four months, and I'm not going to stop because you want me to tell you every detail of my life."

I found my eyes welling up, and within seconds, tears were pouring down my face. I loved Rick, and I truly believed that he had saved my life. I couldn't imagine not speaking to him every day, not meeting with him regularly to go over my steps, or just going out for a meal together before or after a meeting. But I was determined, and nothing was going to change my mind.

Rick looked extremely surprised as I told him this. He had probably expected to reprimand me, and for me to succumb to his direction as I normally did. After all, he had been sober for over seven years longer than me, and he was my role model, the person who had what I wanted when I first met him. But I no longer wanted what he had, and I was sure that I was making the right decision. *At first, he had seemed so kind and peaceful, but now he was resentful and angry.* His kind face looked stricken too, and I felt my heartbreaking inside me.

"If that's what you want," he said sadly. "Thank you for letting me be of service to you. You've helped me more than you know."

I got up to leave. "Thank you for your service," I said. "You have taught me so much. I will be forever indebted to you."

He stood up and put his arms around me, holding me tightly. I felt like I was losing my best friend, but I was angry, and I didn't want to work with him anymore. *I would find a woman who would finish my steps with me, someone maternal and loving.* I left the office before him and got into the elevator. *I hope I didn't make a mistake. This hurts more than breaking up with a boyfriend whom I love but I know is wrong for me.*

An older woman named Eve, with twenty-five years of sobriety, took me on and finished my steps with me one week before my one-year anniversary. When we finished, she told me that she was going away for several months and wouldn't be able to continue sponsoring me. Fortunately, I had met an incredible woman named Sharon who was closer to my age, and a mom, and she agreed to take me on as her sponsee. Since I had finished my steps, she would be available to speak on the phone and to meet with me when I needed guidance with my recovery and my sponsees. She has been my sponsor ever since.

I was now officially ready to sponsor someone else. I had a year sober and had worked my steps. It was time for me to pay it forward as a sponsor for another woman who wanted to get sober and work the steps. A woman named Helene, who was about fifteen years younger than me, and a single mom, had been asking me to sponsor her for a couple of months. She had been sober for seventeen years and had relapsed two years earlier on a sunny beach during a vacation in the Caribbean. Ever since, she had been unable to stay sober.

"How am I going to help you?" I asked her one morning after our home group meeting. "I don't even have a year yet, and I've never sponsored anyone before."

"You have what I want," she said, staring at me with her bespectacled brown eyes. "You're green and excited, and that's what I need to find in my own recovery again." Being green referred to having excitement and bringing new life into the recovery program. I loved A.A. and C.A. and shared about my gratitude for the programs often during meetings and how happy I was to be sober.

After discussing it with Sharon, I agreed to sponsor Helene. I was petrified. I had done the steps, but I barely remembered how. Sharon promised to walk me through the process and answer any questions that I had, which would prove to be plentiful.

Helene called me every day to check in. She never missed a call. We spoke on the phone at length most days. She was going through a difficult divorce, trying to pay the bills for herself and her daughter, and most importantly, desperate to get sober.

"Are you willing to go to any lengths?" I asked, just as my sponsors had asked me.

"Yes," she replied. "Yes, I am."

Helene stayed sober for eighty-four days. On day 85, she called and told me that she had enjoyed a night out with some friends the evening before. "What did you drink?" I asked her.

"Oh, just tonic and bitters," she replied. "It was so lovely. I felt like I was really drinking with my pretty glass."

"What are bitters?" I asked her.

"Oh, they're just something that you put in cocktails. Don't worry."

I looked up bitters online and found that they did contain alcohol. I didn't know what to do, so I called Sharon and explained the situation.

"Bitters are alcohol, babe," she told me. "That's not sober. People in recovery don't drink things with alcohol, and *mocktails* are never a good idea for people like us."

We devised a plan, and during my next call with Helene, we agreed to meet the next morning at our home group (this was a 9:00 a.m. A.A. meeting at 50 Perry that we both went to regularly) and then get together for coffee.

"You know," I told Helene the next day, "bitters do have alcohol in them."

"Yes, I know," she said.

"Do you want to start your day count over?" I asked her.

"Yes," she said, looking completely defeated. "I guess so."

A few minutes later, Helene looked across the table at me.

"You know," she said, "if I have to start counting my days over, I might as well get really drunk first."

This was what I feared would happen, and I didn't want her slip to become a full-blown relapse. She did go out and drink herself into a blackout that night and called me in tears the next morning.

"I'm ready now," she sobbed. "Will you give me another chance?"

I decided to try again, determined to help her. We began her day count over and spoke at length every single day for ninety days. Sometimes we talked for over an hour. Our conversations covered her challenges at work, her divorce proceedings, social interactions, and issues with her daughter.

On day 90, Helene was home in bed. She had been ill for many days and wanted me to come over and meet at her Tribeca apartment.

"Helene," I kept telling her, "I love you, but I really can't afford to get sick right now. We can speak on the phone whenever you want."

She called me again that evening as Mark and I were cabbing to the East Village for dinner with friends.

"I'm so sick," she cried over the phone. "You don't even care about me!"

I was frustrated because I had done nothing but care for her for six months.

"Of course, I care about you, honey," I told her kindly. "I'm so proud of you for getting ninety days! You are a beautiful miracle. Now, Mark and I are on our way out, so get some sleep and we'll talk tomorrow. I love you."

About an hour into our dinner, Helene began blowing my cell phone up with text messages. *I'm drunk,* she wrote, *and it's all because of you.*

Stop drinking, I texted back. *And go to sleep. You're sick, and you need your rest.*

I hate you, and I don't ever want to talk to you or see you again. You care about all the other people at Perry more than me.

Our home group was 50 Perry Street, and I had many friends there, but none of them were more important to me than Helene.

You know that isn't true. You're my special girl.

You're so selfish, she wrote back immediately. *I hate you. Don't ever speak to me again. I drank because of you.*

I was devastated. *I had failed her again… I was a terrible sponsor.* I spoke to Sharon about it the next day.

"I'm the worst sponsor ever," I told her, my eyes tearing. "I should have never sponsored her."

"You were a perfect sponsor, honey," Sharon assured me. "We can't keep anyone sober, nor can we make them drink. She wanted you because she thought she could walk all over you and manipulate you. You're sober, so you did everything right."

"Okay," I said, wiping a tear from my cheek. "Thank you."

Common knowledge in A.A. told us that we were messengers who shared what we had learned from others. We passed our learning along and hoped to shine the light for newcomers. None of us had an original thought—we learned from others, and we passed it on. The Big Book of A.A. outlined the program, and we read the book, worked our steps with a sponsor, and then tried to help others. I had tried and failed miserably. But I had remained sober every day. Sometimes just knowing that Helene would be calling me was enough to stave off a craving. *What would Helene think if I picked up a drink or a drug?* I would ask myself. *She would be so disappointed.*

I have gone on to sponsor many other women. Some of them stay sober, and some of them don't. They are supposed to call me every day. I meet with them weekly to work their steps. They know that they can call me any time of day or night if they have a craving to drink or use. Over time, I have learned not to personalize my sponsees' successes or failures. I'm sober, and that's what Sharon continues to remind me.

Louis Lived in a Sober House in Brooklyn

There was a man named Louis in my Intensive Outpatient group at Hazelden. (Hazelden is a renowned rehab, with inpatient facilities in Minnesota and other states and many IOPs.) Louis was about my age (fifty-one) and followed me around a lot. Outside on the sidewalk during breaks, he lit my cigarettes. He smoked a lot and lit a second cigarette as soon as he finished the first, getting in as many toxins as possible during our short reprieve. When I left at the end of the day, he walked me to the subway sometimes, even though I didn't think he was going the same way. Louis was a pretty big guy—tall and thick, with short receding hair that was mostly gray. He dressed conservatively, in chinos and button-down shirts. He was neither handsome nor unattractive, and there was a kindness and vulnerability in his dark-brown eyes. In my raw and emotional state, I figured he had a crush on me.

I later learned that Louis was gay. He absolutely did not have a crush on me, at least not in the way I had imagined. And Louis was not the only gay man I met in my early recovery whom I mistook as straight. These sober men, I imagined, would hold me, talk to me, protect me, and keep me sober. I was truly crazy in those early days on so many levels, but I was determined to stay sober. The only thing I had to do perfectly, I was told, was to not pick up a drug or a drink.

Louis lived in a sober house. He owned a house on Long Island, but he didn't live there.

"How come you live in a sober house?" I asked one afternoon as we walked down Ninth Avenue together.

"I'm afraid I'll smoke crack if I go home. There's no accountability there."

"How does the sober house keep you accountable?" I asked him.

"They UA us randomly."

We were also given UAs at our IOP. This was the abbreviation used for urine analysis, and it tested for a plethora of drugs. I had no idea what a sober house was, but it sounded absolutely terrible to me. I envisioned a flophouse for dirty, mangy, homeless drug addicts. Whenever Louis mentioned his sober house, I felt pity for him. He seemed to love living there, and one day he announced that he was prolonging his stay there and seemed really happy about it.

I was completely perplexed. Why would somebody with his own house want to keep living in a sober house with other people? I could live in my apartment and stay sober. All my old triggers surrounded me: the bars and restaurants that I drank and used in, the people I drank with, the people I bought drugs from, the people I did drugs with. But I just didn't go into those places any more.

After treatment I would take the subway home and walked into my apartment building through the back door so that none of my old "friends" across the street from my building's front entrance would see me and beckon me in for a quick drink, a coffee, a conversation. When I took a taxi home, I wouldn't let the driver stop across the street from my building even if the light was red and I could save a dollar in wait time. As long as I didn't step foot near my old haunts—Pao, The Ear, Giorgione—I would be able to stay sober.

Louis had been a successful doctor for many years.

"Where did you go to medical school?" I asked Louis during our process group one day.

"Columbia. And I did my residency at Mt. Sinai." He was Ivy League educated and had built up his own practice.

"Wow! I knew you were smart, but that's impressive."

"Did you use while you were treating patients?" one of the other women in our group asked him.

"Yes. I was a very high-functioning crack addict and didn't think that it was negatively impacting my work. I was smoking for seventeen years, and I used at work for about the last six or seven."

"So what happened?" our therapist asked him.

"Someone reported me to the medical board," he said, looking suddenly sad and older than his age. His shoulders slumped down, and he looked at the floor. "I lost my license to practice medicine and was sent away to a treatment center." Louis explained that he had a long road ahead of him if he ever wanted to practice again. For the short term, he hoped that he might be allowed to teach at his alma mater.

Now after several months abstinent and in therapy, he was recognizing the mess that his life had become. He was broke and unemployable at the age of fifty. He felt safe at his sober house because he knew he couldn't get high and stay there. He had a lot at stake.

One day after group, Louis was walking me to my subway stop.

"Hey," he said, "I'm speaking at my sober house next week for my ninety days."

"Cool," I replied, a bit jealous. Having not gone to inpatient myself, I had a mere forty-three days' clean. I was already looking forward to the day when I could tell my ninety-day story.

"I'd like you to come."

What? I thought, horrified. *Go to his sober house in Brooklyn? Was he kidding me?* I could barely make it home after group. Staying sober was not easy, and the thought of going to Brooklyn alone terrified me.

"When are you speaking?" I asked.

Maybe I could be busy at that time (not that I had any plans whatsoever). My plans were meetings, work, treatment, dinner with my son and perhaps my husband, then under the covers with my dog and my cell phone until it was time to go to sleep. Mark still drank, and that was difficult for me, so I often encouraged him to stay out or to watch TV in the living room until he was ready to go to sleep.

"Thursday night," he said. "The meeting starts at seven thirty. And you can eat dinner at the house with us first if you want."

Eat dinner at the sober house? Was he kidding me? I envisioned beef stew made out of tough fatty meat, with soft-cooked carrots and mushy potatoes. He gave me the details, and I told him I would let him know.

I told my sponsor about the invitation that night during our daily phone call.

"That's amazing, Mallory!" he told me. "You have to go! That is doing service."

Showing up for another person in recovery—that is what I was supposed to do. I heard it in meetings all the time. My sponsor talked about it constantly. If Louis was speaking at a morning or afternoon meeting in Manhattan, I would show up, I told my sponsor. But Brooklyn? Nighttime?

I stressed out about this a lot, but I forced myself to go. Tearing myself away from the safety of my Soho loft, my sober dachshund Grandpa, and my adorable son, I took the subway to Brooklyn, fearful for my sobriety and my safety. Thinking back on it today, I realized that I was just fearful of going anywhere without my best friends: drugs and alcohol. They always made me feel thinner, prettier, more interesting, less socially anxious. Without them, I felt completely exposed, as if I had left my apartment and forgotten to wear a bra beneath my skintight tank top. And I *never* left the house braless.

I reached the address after walking several blocks past twentysomethings reading poetry and drinking beers. The elevator opened into a beautiful loft where a chef was preparing dinner in an industrial kitchen. Louis came out to greet me and show me around.

"Let me give you a tour," he offered.

The bedrooms had full-size beds with Ralph Lauren comforters. The floors were hardwood, the bathrooms clean and modern. The living room had plush leather couches and armchairs, a big wooden coffee table in the center. It was homey and comfortable, a truly beautiful loft. It was the complete antithesis of what I had expected—cheap cots, threadbare furnishings.

"This is beautiful," I said, trying not to reveal my shock.

There were bowls with snacks all around: fresh fruit, packets of nuts, granola bars. The chef had created several dishes for everyone, and people were eating various selections from the dinner meal. There was grilled salmon, asparagus, roasted chicken, rice, fresh berries, freshly baked cookies, and more. I had some salad and arrived with my trusty bottle of Fiji water, which was always on hand since I had put down alcohol.

The residents, men and women, ranged in age from early twenties to late fifties. They all seemed like normal people, rather than the down-and-out addicts I had devised in my mind. It was an upscale A.A. meeting in their sober house, and everyone was articulate and supportive of Louis after he told his story of how he had made it to ninety days without a crack pipe, one day at a time.

I was almost sad when I left. It seemed comforting to live among other people in early recovery while I was returning home to my husband who drank every day and my children who didn't know I was sick. My son was in his junior year of high school, and my daughter had recently started college away from home. I attended meetings and IOP primarily while my son was at school or busy with sports and friends, and he was used to me having a sporadic schedule, since I had been working as a real estate agent for thirteen years.

I called my sponsor Rick when I got home. "The sober house was amazing. I would love to open one someday."

"And someday maybe you shall, my dear," he replied. "How many days sober do you have today?"

"I have fifty-two days today."

"You're a miracle."

"You saved my life," I said, as I always did. He hated when I said that.

"No," he reminded me, like a tape playing over and over again, "I just shone the light for you like it was shone for me."

"How can I ever repay you?" I asked him, overwhelmed by his kindness and guidance. Nobody had ever given so freely of themselves to me before without expecting something back in return.

"You already are," he reminded me. "Showing up for Louis tonight was doing service. Helping newcomers is doing service. You're helping me more than I'm helping you."

This was a concept that I didn't really understand yet, though I heard it said often in C.A. and A.A. meetings.

"Just pay it forward for someone else whenever you can," he said. "That's the way we do it here."

He had already explained to me that buying him dinner or the little gifts I had been surprising him with was not something that was expected or even wanted in the program. It was not about material things. It was about saving another person's life by sharing our experiences with them. Only an addict truly understands another addict, and only recovering addicts can provide the direction and counsel that I so desperately needed. It was the simplest and most beautiful thing I had ever encountered. No psychiatrist or friend had been able to remove my obsession to do coke, but the minute I stepped foot in a C.A. meeting and met Rick I found what I had been looking for all those years. Rick was seven years sober from cocaine and alcohol, and he was happy, joyous, and free. We were nothing alike—and yet exactly the same. He gave me hope that had never existed before, and I promised myself that I would pay it forward for the rest of my life, one day at a time.

Resentments Are the
Biggest Offender

Before I got sober, I was disappointed in a lot of people. Somehow I always expected others to behave the way I wanted them to, and when they didn't, I felt extremely let down.

When I worked Step Four with my sponsor, I was instructed to write a list of people I had resentments toward and then to describe what I was upset about, how it affected me, and what my part was. After about a month, Rick asked me how my list was going.

"I'm still writing it," I told him.

"How many people are on it so far?" he asked me over the phone.

"Thirty-nine," I told him proudly.

"Stop now!" he said. "Are *you* on the list?"

"No."

"Add yourself and then let's set up a meeting to review what you have."

"But there are still a couple of people that I need to include," I told him. "I have huge resentments about them."

"Two more," he insisted.

So when we sat down to discuss my resentments, there were forty-two people on the list. *No wonder I had done drugs. I was disappointed in everyone in my life and even some people who had died.*

As Rick and I reviewed this list (which took a total of seven hours over three meetings), a common theme arose. If I did something nice for someone, I expected him or her to do something nice for me.

"Expectations are resentments waiting to happen," Rick explained. "They will bring you back to a drink or a drug every time."

This made total sense to me. If I bought my husband a card and a gift for Valentine's Day, and he didn't have roses or something special to give me back, I was hurt. Eventually divorce seemed inevitable. If I told him that I loved him, and he didn't say it back immediately, I felt needy and unloved. I would say it over and over until he finally said it back. Everything I did seemed to have an expectation attached to it. I ended relationships over these things, believing that I was better off alone than being unappreciated.

I expected my parents to love my children the way I thought Jewish grandparents should love them, and when they didn't step up, I was crushed. The day Morgan was born, my parents were at the hospital in Manhattan waiting to hold her. They seemed to be madly in love with her, and I hoped that bringing her into the world would bring all of us closer.

When Morgan was three months old, my parents bought a home in Las Vegas and sold their home on Long Island. I couldn't believe that they were moving. The only time they returned to New York in over twenty years was for three nights after Jack was born. My dad showed up at our Tribeca loft every morning to hold baby Jack, but my mom was back at their hotel with diarrhea. She wanted to cut their trip short so she could be sick in the comfort of her own home, but flying across the country with diarrhea seemed even worse, so they stayed the full three days.

For many years, I flew to Las Vegas with my young chil-dren, hoping to please my parents. It didn't work. Staying at their home quickly became a nightmare, and we started staying in hotels. The amount of time that my parents spent with my children got shorter and shorter, and I realized that the expense and effort of bringing them to Las Vegas was making my parents unhappy, rather than providing them with the joy I had hoped for. Although my parents never liked and loved me the way I expected, I had been sure that my beautiful children would change all that.

I was wrong, and my parents began to find fault with my children, their father, and the way I was parenting. I listened to my friends telling stories of extended family vacations with their parents, siblings, and grandchildren in tow. I compared families and felt disappointed in my parents and siblings for not adoring my children the way that I did. I was heartbroken.

"Don't ever have children," my parents told me and my brothers over dinner one night before any of us were grown. "Just enjoy your own lives."

What did that even mean? I had wanted my own children from the time I was old enough to even contemplate being a mother. *I would love and cherish my own children the way I wished I had been,* I promised myself.

"What are you saying?" I asked my parents. "That you wish you hadn't had us?"

"Of course not, Mallory," my father replied, speaking dismissively. "Don't be silly. It's just that children are expensive, and once you have them, they are always there."

Exactly, and that's what I want! There is nothing that I have done in my lifetime that has given me more pride and joy than mothering Morgan and Jack. I cannot wait to be a grandmother—one who babysits and vacations with and spoils my grandchildren rotten. My brothers never had children, and they definitely have more disposable income than I do, but I wouldn't trade being a mother with anything in the world.

Rick taught me how to look at my part in all my resentments. I was always doing something with the expectation of getting something in return. In the 12-step program, we are taught that we are supposed to do things for others without expectations. The Saint Francis prayer tells us:

Where there is hatred, let me bring love…

let me not seek as much…

to be consoled as to console,

to be loved than to love,

for it is in giving that one receives,

it is in pardoning that one is pardoned…

By working the 12-steps with a sponsor, we learn how to be more forgiving and loving—less selfish and more selfless. I didn't come into the program to become a better person. I came in to save my life. What I found was so much more. When I develop resentments today, I look at my part and work through the feelings immediately. I have learned to think before I speak. I try to ask myself *Is it true? Is it nice? Is it necessary?* before I speak or text. We cannot take away something once it is written and sent to another, or after we have spoken. It is easier to pause first, trying not to inflict harm on others. When I find myself in a pointless argument I try to remember *I'd rather be happy than right.* These are tools that I have learned from others in meetings.

In the morning, upon awakening, I remind myself to think, *Thank you for waking me up today. Please keep me sober today. Please help me to be of service. Please help me to be the kindest person I can be today.* I ask to be filled with kind thoughts, words, and feelings. The more I live this way, the less I need to make amends and to right the wrongs that I have committed. Before bed each night, I am told to do a daily inventory and to make amends if I have acted poorly.

Having low expectations or no expectations is something that I have learned to strive for. When I do something for someone, I try to do it with clear motives. For so long, I tried to manipulate others with my actions, and the results were nil. We are told that we don't go to a dry well to drink, and I realize today that certain people are not going to live up to my ideals, so I have stopped trying to change them and their behaviors.

I wake up joyful, excited to meet a new day—grateful to be alive and sober. I try to be of service to others. My goal is to be mindful and present. We cannot change even one second of the past, so I strive to move beyond negative experiences, to learn from them rather than wallow in regret and negativity. I make an effort not to future trip because I have no idea how things are going to turn out. I know that I cannot read other people's minds and that things are going to turn out the way they are meant to. When things don't go my way, I accept them and believe that something better is around the corner.

Meeting Makers Make It

"Meeting makers make it, and service givers keep it," I heard in meetings when I was counting my first ninety days sober.

"What does that even mean?" I asked Rick.

"It means that people who go to meetings get sober, and people who do service stay sober."

"What is service?"

The program was completely foreign to me, and there was much I didn't understand. Sometimes I felt like I was in a class filled with people speaking a foreign language that only I didn't understand.

"Chairing meetings, going to business meetings, sharing in meetings, being a sponsor—anything to pay it forward to the fellowship."

Because I was desperate to stay sober, I wanted to do everything right. Rick introduced me to business meetings during my first month, and this was where elections were held. When I had eighty-four days sober, elections were being held at a 6:00 p.m. C.A. meeting. The position of secretary was open for Friday nights, and the requirement to serve for this position was ninety days. It was a six-month commitment.

"Who wants to nominate themselves for this position?" the chairperson asked.

By Friday, I would have eighty-seven days sober—just three days short. If they would vote me in, I would be likely to stay sober for the next six months. *Service givers keep it,* I thought.

Three hands shot up—one of them was mine.

"I'll have eighty-seven days on Friday," I said. "But I want a service commitment."

e chair asked the three of us to leave the room while d. The other two people had a lot more time than as certain that I would lose. Waiting felt like it went minutes, but it was probably no more than three. ack in," somebody said, opening the door.

of us filed back in.

the new secretary," the chair said.

lieve it! The room clapped for my win, and I h them. *I can't believe I won. I'm so excited!*

For the next six months, I arrived a bit early to the 6:00 p.m. C.A. meeting and sat next to the chairperson. Midway through the meeting I read the secretary's script, "There are no dues or fees for C.A. membership, we are self-supporting through our own contributions..."

I passed the basket around the room, but I wasn't allowed to count the money. I felt so important and connected when I stood up to read my little section. A few weeks into my tenure, my sponsor told me that I wasn't supposed to stand when I read. I was totally embarrassed. I was so thrilled to be a part of this fellowship that was saving my life that I had been prancing around like a B actress on a stage. By the time I was about six months sober, I humbled myself, reading the script from my seat. Today when I watch new people standing, it brings a reflective smile to my face. *That was me,* I think fondly.

Here are some of the places where I have been to meetings—Manhattan, Long Island, Delray Beach, Islamorada, Boca, Boynton Beach, West Palm Beach, Brooklyn, Red Hook, Rhinebeck, Las Vegas, Savannah, Naples, Charleston, Vero Beach, Ocklawaha, Boston, and Nashville. Whenever I travel, I google meetings before I leave home. I make sure that I stay in close proximity to meetings and plan my schedule around them. Traveling can be especially triggering for alcoholics and addicts. We can tell ourselves that drinking doesn't count if we're flying on an airplane, sailing on a cruise ship, or visiting a place where nobody knows us. *Who would know?* our addictive brains ask us. It is essential that we learn to be accountable for ourselves. Intergroup websites have listings of meetings, and I call ahead to make sure the addresses and times are correct.

Sometimes on vacations I chase meetings. One morning in Boston, I woke early to attend a sunrise meeting. I walked there from my hotel, toting a big Chanel bag. When I arrived, I was the only woman and the only white person amidst a big group of homeless black men. *It's okay,* I told myself. *We're all here for the same reason.* We stood outside in line, waiting for the doors to be unlocked. The longer we waited, the more unwelcome I felt. I didn't have a problem with them, but they didn't seem to want me. They were staring me down, and nobody returned my smile—I became frightened for my own safety. I quickly checked my phone and found a meeting across town that was starting at

8:15 a.m. I hailed a cab and remembered. I had been to this meeting before.

"Welcome back," one of the men at the conference table said to me. My heart rate began to return to normal within moments.

There were little farm animals on the table. They had given me a tiny cow the last time I visited. Cows and frogs are my favorite animals, and I had stowed my baby cow along with all my other coins. "There are no strangers here," one of my visitor's coins read. "Just friends we have never met."

On our drive down to Florida from New York City, I wouldn't let Mark stop for a Starbucks one day. We were heading into Savannah, Georgia, and if I missed the late-afternoon meeting, I wouldn't be able to go to a meeting until very late at night—something I wasn't comfortable doing.

"I'm so thirsty," Mark said.

"Please!" I begged him, "Just get a coffee after you drop me at the meeting!" We made it into town with time to spare. I dropped Mark at the hotel and drove over to the meeting. There was a beautiful rainbow over a small bridge as I made my way there. *It was meant to be.*

I always felt better when I went to a meeting. Sometimes I felt anxious—at other times triggered. At home wherever I sat, after about ten minutes in my chair, the feelings would lift and I began to feel lighter. *I have earned this seat. I'm going to hold on to it.*

"How far did you go for a drink or a drug when you were out there?" people ask in meetings. I remember times when I chased drugs—in New York, Jamaica, Puerto Rico, Las Vegas, Florida, Los Angeles. Some of my vacations were ruined while I ran around trying to find a connection rather than enjoying the place where I was staying and the people I was with. Finding meetings was much easier than finding drugs, and I knew what I would get. Coke is being mixed with fentanyl now, which kills people. I have never heard of anyone dying from an A.A. meeting.

The first time Mark and I visited my dad in Las Vegas after I stopped drinking and drugging, I was desperate to find a meeting near my hotel.

"I need to rent a car," I told Mark. "I have to go to a meeting every day."

I was worried about this trip. It was taking place during my birthday, and I hadn't experienced a birthday sober in over thirty years. To me, Las Vegas was a city of delicious food and wine, gambling, shopping, and shows. I didn't know how I was going to stay sober during this five-day stint.

I raised my hand at 50 Perry Street a few days before I was leaving.

"I'm going to Las Vegas to see my dad, and I'm worried about relapsing," I shared. "I haven't been sober around my father in about thirty years, and it's my birthday." I was hoping that someone would have some advice.

A regular named David at the meeting raised his hand right after I finished sharing.

"I'm going to Las Vegas this week too," he said, looking me right in the eye. "Maybe we can go to some meetings together."

After the meeting, we exchanged phone numbers. I found a clubhouse near my hotel, and we agreed to meet there every morning. It's called Serenity Club, and they hold meetings from early morning until late at night.

"I have free passes to a really cool club tomorrow night for my birthday," I told David after our morning meeting in Vegas the second day. "Do you want to come with me?" I was petrified at the thought of going to a nightclub sober.

"Sure," he said.

The club was at the Encore. David brought his friend Christopher with him. Christopher was covered with tattoos—he even had them on his eyelids. He was kind of gorgeous, with big muscles and a beautiful face. "Do you have any tattoos on your stomach?" I asked him in the lobby of the hotel.

"Yep."

"Can I see?"

Christopher lifted his shirt, exposing a chest covered with tattoos and pierced nipples with thick silver rings coming out. Just looking at them hurt me. Mark looked mortified, but I was having fun.

We entered the club through the VIP entrance. Our frequent visits to Las Vegas had afforded us some privileges. The club was dark, the music loud. Beautiful go-go dancers were everywhere, wearing tiny shorts and miniskirts, sporting perfect bodies. A DJ was spinning amazing songs, and colored lights were flashing.

I felt completely uncomfortable. Mark bought us all drinks. He and Christopher got alcohol, but David ordered a soda, and I got sparkling water with a wedge of lime. David started dancing right away. I was wearing a short, skintight dress and six-inch heels. I could hardly move.

"How can you dance sober?" I asked David, shouting in his ear.

"I just can," he said, showing off his moves. David had gotten sober five years before me.

I didn't dance that night, but Mark was kind. He walked around with me. All I could focus on was what everyone else was drinking or taking. I knew if I were high or drinking, I would be dancing too, but without anything to alter my mind, I was self-conscious in a way I didn't remember being before.

"I want to go up to the room," I told Mark about forty-five minutes after we arrived.

"No problem."

I said goodbye to David and Christopher. David was dancing like a wild man on ecstasy. We agreed to meet at our A.A. meeting the next morning. Getting into the elevator to return to my room had never felt better. I looked at my watch. It was 12:15 a.m. I made it through my first sober birthday!

There is an unwritten code about getting to know meeting people in A.A. that lets us feel that we can be honest and open. "We are only as sick as our secrets," we hear in meetings, and "sharing something with another person cuts it in half."

I met Bob at an A.A. meeting in Rhinebeck early one morning. I was visiting Morgan at Bard and going to my home away from home every morning. I had just gotten out of my Mercedes SUV as Bob was getting out of his BMW SUV. We were both carrying hot coffees from the same place, trying to wake up and warm up simultaneously.

"Hey," he said, flashing his big white smile.

"Hey." He was gorgeous. Blond, tall, and beautifully built.

Midway through the meeting Bob got up to refresh his coffee in the open kitchen, and I joined him.

"How long have you been sober?" I asked him.

He looked at me and then looked down. Immediately I saw pain and despair.

"One day."

"Crystal meth?" I asked him.

He looked surprised, and on closer inspection, I noticed the dark circles underneath his blue eyes.

"Yes."

"We'll talk after the meeting."

Bob lived in the city too and had a weekend place near Rhinebeck that he shared with his husband of many years. He was struggling badly, and I invited him to join me at a C.A. meeting back in the city that week. We exchanged numbers and became immediate friends. Rick became his sponsor. I had learned in C.A. that many of the gay men who were crystal methamphetamine addicts were more successful in C.A. than CMA (Crystal Meth Anonymous). Many of the CMA meetings in Manhattan bred dates, drugs, and ultimately unprotected sex. C.A. seemed to be a safer bet.

Bob started to join me at A.A. and C.A. meetings in the city. It was a crazy feeling to see familiar faces in meetings wherever I went. We all flocked to the same places to maintain our sobriety for one more day. Seeing a familiar face in a strange place is comforting, and I have experienced this many times.

Some people don't like meetings, and I feel sorry for them. Almost every time I hear about a relapse or a drug- or alcohol-linked death, I find out that the person had stopped going to meetings. An hour a day is a very small price to pay for my continued sobriety. My life today is fantastic because I found the program. I'm too scared to give it up. Meetings make me happy—a feeling I chased with drugs and alcohol for years. Instead of chasing drugs today, I choose to chase meetings. I want to be happy, joyous, and free, and A.A. tells me that I will be all of those if I keep coming back.

At the end of my meeting every single day, I hold hands in a circle with other people who are treating their disease like I do. "Keep coming back. It works if you work it." *So work it, you're worth it, and live it,* I add silently, remembering those additional words from my New York City meetings. I am so happy to be alive and sober today, and I give all the credit to the program.

I have learned to do things that I enjoy and to compete only with myself. I want to spin better than I did last week— to master a new pose in yoga. Looking at those around me doesn't matter anymore. Now it's how I feel that I focus on. Competing with myself is enough for me today.

I got married four times. Every guy seemed like the answer to my problems. I would meet him and write a screenplay in my mind. He would ask me to marry him, presenting me with a beautiful diamond engagement ring. We would plan a wedding and honeymoon. He would take care of me and fill up the emptiness that was always inside me.

Two years into the marriage I looked at the man lying next to me in bed and wondered what I was doing with him. Nothing had changed. I was still empty inside—lonely even when I wasn't alone.

Recovery has changed all this. My fourth husband, Mark, is perfect just the way he is. He doesn't fill me up. He's just a man whom I choose to love. He allows me to be sober and to explore the parts of me that I want to explore. He is happy inside, and so am I. And so together, we are perfect just the way we are. We have been together for almost nine years now, and I plan to grow old with him. The only thing that has really changed is my perspective.

Sucking at things doesn't even enter my brain any more. I don't need to be better than anyone else. I just need to be okay as I am right now.

Don't Worry, You Can Live at My House

By the time I moved to Florida full-time, Mark and I were empty nesters. I missed the daily companionship of my children. Morgan had been away at college for two years, and I had just dropped Jack off at Boston University, when I felt a real sense of loss. After twenty years with children in the house, things were too quiet. Mark was spending half of his time in New York, so I was truly alone much of time.

I got a new sponsee named Kayla at the 7:00 a.m. meeting that I went to almost every day. She was young and beautiful. She was living in a coed sober house after a month in treatment. Her boyfriend, Tony, who was wealthy and much older than her, was footing the bill.

"What are you doing today?" I asked her after the meeting the first day that I met her.

"Nothing," she said.

"Don't you need to get a job so you can start paying for your sober house and food?"

"Yes, I do," she told me.

"It's really easy to find a job down here," I told her. "You should go out and start filling in applications. Do you have a resume?"

"Yes, but I need to print it out. Do you have a printer I could use?"

I did have a printer, but I didn't believe in doing things like this for my sponsees.

"You can go to the library or Office Depot to print it out," I told her.

Kayla didn't look for a job that day, or the next. She called me each afternoon at five. She didn't seem to be doing much other than hanging out with her roommate and spending time with a younger guy named Billy who lived at her sober house. I reminded her that she had a boyfriend and he was paying all her bills.

"I know," she sighed, "but Billy is so much younger, and he's so hot. Tony is such an old man."

"If you want to be with Billy, you should break up with Tony," I told her.

"No, I'm not going to break up with him. He took me to rehab and picked me up. He loves me, and I love him so much."

"You have too much free time on your hands," I reminded her. "How many jobs have you applied to this week?"

"None."

Kayla had been going to the beach and to the gym with her roommate and Billy. She was sober though and attended the early meeting every day. My primary purpose as her sponsor was to help her stay sober and work the steps with her.

"I want you to find a job today," I told Kayla after the 7:00 a.m. meeting about a week after we had met. I had been buying her coffee at Starbucks and had paid for her lunch the day we met to discuss her history and to get to know one another better. I gave her a list of three places to apply to.

"I got a job!" she told me that afternoon. "I went to the first place you recommended, and they hired me on the spot!"

"That's great!"

She would be making nine dollars an hour. She had a college degree from a good school and had held much better jobs in the past, but for now she needed structure and a regular paycheck. She was thirty-three years old and didn't have a dollar to her name. Her family was done helping her.

She didn't have health insurance, a car, or a driver's license. All she had was her sobriety and a roof over her head.

Kayla started working and was very happy to have a job. She was a cashier at a burger joint, but it was something. Billy and her roommate were dropping her off and picking her up.

A few days into her job, Kayla called me.

"I got kicked out of my sober house!" she cried. "I don't know what to do."

"What happened?"

"I took Billy into my room to watch a movie, and we got caught. He's getting kicked out also. And I don't have any money to go somewhere else. Tony won't pay for me to move somewhere else. He's so angry with me. I told him that Billy and I are just friends, but he told me that it's my mess and I have to figure it out."

Kayla was sobbing now, and she was having trouble breathing. I could barely understand what she was saying. "They kicked me out!" she repeated. "I'm standing on the street with all of my stuff. I have nowhere to go."

"Don't worry," I told her. "You can stay at my house until you figure things out."

Billy drove Kayla over. She had enough designer clothing, shoes, and handbags to fill an upscale consignment
shop. I put her in a spare bedroom and told her to be ready
to go to the 7:00 a.m. meeting with me the next morning.
She was up and dressed by 6:30 a.m., and I bought her a
Starbucks on the way to the meeting. She put a bottle of water
on the counter too, so I paid for that as well. She wouldn't
have a paycheck until she had worked for a full two weeks.

Billy was staying at hotels. He had been kicked out of
multiple sober houses, and his parents always paid to bail
him out of his troubles. I was just glad that Kayla wasn't staying with him so that I could keep an eye on her. Kayla was
constantly on Facebook and Instagram, stalking Tony and
Billy, and taking suggestive selfies, which she posted non-
stop. Every time I walked past her sitting in my living room,
she wanted to show me some guy who had commented on
her latest posts.

"Kayla," I reminded her, "you have work to do on your
first step. You need to work on that during your free time and
stop playing with your phone all the time."

Kayla ate with us every night. She would accompany me
to the supermarket, throwing all the groceries she wanted

into my shopping cart. Mark and I paid for everything, and we ate out often. I felt bad leaving her at home alone, so she became my constant companion when she wasn't at work.

One night I left her alone because Mark was getting sick of eating out with her every night. When we got home, she was gone.

Where are you? I texted her.

I'm at Billy's hotel watching a movie.

Somehow watching a movie sounded more like having sex to me. When I asked her about this, she admitted that they were having sex, but watching movies too.

"I have such a high sex drive, and Tony's such an old man. I love Billy's body, and he's obsessed with me. He makes me feel so sexy."

Kayla continued to beg Tony for money while she was running around with Billy. Tony paid for important things, like doctor's appointments, but he wasn't giving her any money for rent or groceries.

My children came to visit over Thanksgiving, and Kayla was like a third child though she was thirty-three years old. She loved Morgan and Jack, and though they were only twenty and eighteen, her maturity level was close to theirs.

She invited Billy over multiple times and confided in my son Jack about her relationship woes.

"She's a slut," Jack told me one night. He seemed disappointed in Kayla and had better values than she did. I questioned myself for having her at our house. It was over a month since she had moved in. She told him that she had sex with Billy without a condom and was afraid that she might be pregnant. I was furious with Kayla and told her that she needed to have boundaries with Jack.

"He's so gorgeous," she said. "I wish he was a little older."

I was appalled, and Jack was tiring of Kayla's attempts to massage his shoulders while he was watching TV with her.

"When are you getting paid?" I asked her. "You need to find another sober house to move into."

"I got my first paycheck, and it was only a hundred and ninety-two dollars." She still hadn't chipped in for groceries or paid for a Starbucks for me. I didn't even know she had been paid.

"What did you do with the money?" I asked her.

"I took Billy out for a really nice lunch during my break the other day, and I had to give him money for gas. We had sushi at a really good place. Also, I needed some skin products, so I got a bunch of stuff at Ulta."

The next time Kayla got paid, she came home with a bag of lingerie. "Look what I bought!" she said excitedly. Kayla had a perfect little body, and she loved to show it off. At the age of thirty-three, she had already lured men into paying for a boob job, a nose job, and lots of Botox. She began unwrapping bras and thongs. There were eight of each. I was completely annoyed. *Why didn't she think that she should give Mark and me some money for food? Didn't she realize that we were basically supporting her?*

"Did you really need that many?" I asked.

She pouted. "I haven't gotten new bras and panties in so long," she explained. "And I got injections in my lips! Don't they look amazing?" Her pout did seem more pronounced than usual.

"It's what's on the inside that you need to focus on, Kayla," I told her. "You're fine on the outside. I used to want to have plastic surgery all the time before I got sober, but now I feel like I'm okay just the way I am. You don't need all of this work."

I asked Kayla to buy me a coffee at Starbucks the next day, telling her that I would wait outside in the car. My resentments were building, and I knew that wasn't a good thing. Kayla had been complaining about her hair and how she needed a good haircut and some highlights.

"Kick her out, honey," Sharon told me on the phone later that day. "She's a taker. She goes from one kind soul to another. She doesn't care about anyone but herself."

I suggested to Kayla that she ask her boyfriend to pay for her to live in another sober house. "It's so expensive!" she said. "But I'll ask him." His answer was no.

Kayla went to Billy's hotel to watch another movie (somehow I didn't think they were watching anything other than her posing in her new lingerie). When she got home, she ran up to my room.

"I found needles in his room!" she cried. "He's shooting up! I knew something was wrong. He's been so strange lately."

"Kayla," I said, "you're making some very bad choices. You've been bringing Billy over here, and I don't trust him. I don't want him in my house or near my children." Billy was twenty-three years old. His life was one big vacation, and when he did go to A.A. meetings, he sat silently in the back. He didn't have a sponsor or work the steps.

"He's so hot!" she reminded me for the hundredth time. "I can't believe he's been lying to me!"

"You need to find another place to live. You can't stay here much longer."

Kayla moved in with Tony, her sixty-five-year-old boyfriend. She was fired from her job and did nothing but seduce her boyfriend and try to get him to pay for injections and plastic surgery, manicures, pedicures, and hair treatments. When she relapsed, I asked her to find another sponsor.

Unfortunately, my experiences in bringing recovering women to live at my house have all ended badly. I sometimes refer to myself as *The Eternal Optimist*, and I want to believe in people and to always put my hand out when someone is in need. I'm just not so sure any more that I want to offer my family home. Not one woman who has lived with us has made amends to me or my family, financial or otherwise.

Mommy, I Have a Problem

My daughter, Morgan, is the female love of my life. From the moment she was born, I was madly in love with her. I always dreamed of having a little girl of my own, and she was even better than anything I had ever imagined. Morgan was born on May 5, 1994, and I called her my "Margarita Girl," in honor of Cinco de Mayo, coupled with my love for frozen margaritas with salt.

Being pregnant was not something that I enjoyed. I couldn't drink, or snort cocaine, and I resented that. I remember a dinner out with another couple in Tribeca where I was actually raging inside because everyone could drink except me. Morning sickness did not apply to me—I was nauseated all the time, unless I was sleeping or had food in my mouth. During my sixth month, my belly button herniated, and I could not stand up unless I wore a tight girdle around my stomach. This only added to my already-negative feelings about pregnancy. I wanted this baby more than anything, but I hated the way I looked and felt. I would stand naked in front of my full-length mirror and obsess about the changes that my body was undergoing. I was not one of those glowing mothers-to-be. In fact, my pallor was green.

"Why can't they just put me to sleep until I give birth?" I asked my husband often. "This sucks!" I also wondered why we needed to grow babies inside us when modern medicine did so many cool things. I wished that my baby could grow inside an incubator, and I could just check in on it occasionally.

When Morgan popped out, though, all these things were forgotten. She was perfect in every way. She had a full head of hair and looked like she had just come out of the baby beauty parlor. *How did that grow inside of me?* Her tiny fingernails and toenails amazed me, as did her beautiful little ears and lips. When she was placed in my arms for the first time, she looked me in the eyes and seemed to say, "There you are! I know you." Having Morgan was a miracle like I had never experienced. *How did this perfect little person come out of me? This is truly a gift like no other.* I knew that everyone on the planet had been created the same way, but it felt like I had performed a miracle. The negative feelings that I had endured for almost nine months were immediately forgotten as I basked in the joys of motherhood.

Morgan was the best baby ever. She slept well, ate plentifully, and laughed with joy. She was alert and happy, and I never wanted to leave her side. She didn't want to leave mine either. We were best friends from the first moment we met, and as she grew, her attachment to me got stronger and stronger. When I went out for a run, Morgan stood by the elevator of our Tribeca loft and cried. Her nanny Joy was fantastic, and Morgan loved her too, but Morgan still wanted her mommy.

"Mommy," she asked me when she was two and I was putting her to bed one night, "are you going to die before I die?" She looked at me with her big brown eyes, and I couldn't believe that such a little person was asking such a big question.

"Probably," I told her truthfully. "Usually people who are older die first, but don't worry, I'm not going anywhere for a very long time."

"But I don't want to live if you're not alive," she told me seriously, beginning to cry.

I held my little daughter in my arms, trying to comfort her. Surely most two-year-olds weren't asking about death, so why was mine?

Our nanny Joy held Morgan all the time, and she got used to it. It became very difficult for her to fall asleep by herself. Most nights I read to her in her bed and held her until she finally went to sleep. As silently as possible, I tried to sneak out of her room. "Mommy!" she would often say. "Where are you going? I need you!" Often it was easier to just fall asleep beside her, waking at some point during the night and trying to escape to my own bed.

By six every morning, she would be in our bed. If the door were closed, she banged on it, awakening my husband and me. We had to let her in or she banged relentlessly, and God forbid if we tried to have sex—one night she got a small baseball bat and hit it against the door until we let her in. It was almost a miracle that we had a second child two years later, as Morgan seemed to have a sixth sense when it came to us trying to procreate.

Morgan started kindergarten without a problem. While all the other five-year-olds clung to their parents at drop-off, crying and screaming, Morgan walked in with confidence.

"Bye, Mommy," she said with a proud smile. "See you later."

A week later, while the other children were walking in gladly, Morgan started to panic.

"Mommy! Don't go, Mommy!" she screamed, holding on to me in the yard. "Take me home!"

This continued daily for over a week. Morgan came home from school and cried until bedtime, begging me not to leave her alone at school. Mornings were horrendous—she woke up as early as 5:00 a.m. and started crying about going to school. I was a wreck. I asked Joy to come in early so she could drop Morgan at school. After three years of preschool, I was not prepared for this. I was a nervous wreck, dreading Morgan's cries and complaints. Her teacher said that nothing was wrong at school, and Morgan had no specific complaints.

I went to a child psychiatrist to deal with my anxiety this time. Morgan had been to see her in the past, but I found myself unable to work productively during the day, dreading my almost-sleepless nights and hours of misery trying to calm my little girl down. She prescribed me Paxil, an anti-anxiety medication.

At lunchtime, I found myself walking past the playground at PS234, spying on Morgan. While all her classmates played happily, Morgan sat with her teacher, watching the other children from a distance. Why wasn't she engaging with her friends? I worried.

Morgan had friends, but she was very selective. She loved having children over, or playing in the park after school, but she didn't like to go to other children's homes unless Joy or I stayed with her. Sleepovers at other people's homes were rare, unless they were with Eve, who was Morgan's best friend since infancy. Eve's mother, Brooke, read to Morgan, sometimes for an hour or more after Eve was sleeping peacefully.

Cool boys were very appealing to my daughter, and she played with boys often. She followed them around the local parks, running around and laughing. She played kissing games with them on summer camp buses, and often told more than one boy at a time that she loved them.

In middle school, Morgan "fell in love" with a handsome dark Brazilian boy, and they spent hours on the phone together at night. *She's going to be a real heartbreaker*, I thought.

"I think Morgan's a lesbian," her dad told me on the phone one night, shortly after Morgan, at fourteen, had started high school at Bard High School / Early College. Bard was a gifted program, and many of the children there were gay or bisexual.

"You're crazy," I told him. "Morgan has loved boys since she was a little girl." Her dad and I had separated when Morgan was eight and Jack was six, and we were divorced a year later.

"Your father called me yesterday and said the weirdest thing to me," I told Morgan as we were cooking dinner together the following evening.

"What did he say?"

"He thinks you're gay," I told her. Although Morgan had cut her beautiful, long brown hair to her shoulders shortly after starting at Bard, I still thought of her as a girl who *liked* boys.

"Well, *duh*," she replied casually.

"What do you mean?"

"You're like the last person to know, Mom," she said.

"What? You're telling me you're a lesbian?" *This was impossible. I had never seen a single sign, and Morgan was my best friend. How could I be the last to know?* "When did you realize this?"

"Probably when I was seven," she said.

"So what was the deal with your boyfriend in middle school?"

"His sister was hot."

I thought that it was a phase. So many kids at Bard were gay. Maybe Morgan was just trying to fit in.

Right after our conversation, Morgan cut her hair shorter than Jack's. She started wearing baggy boy's clothing and refused to shop in women's stores. If we went to a coed store, she would immediately charge toward the men's section, refusing to try on anything made for a woman. The result was that she looked heavy, and somewhat androgynous. She had large breasts, which she started hiding, and the shapeless men's clothing she wore made her look like a chubby boy.

"Where do your boys go to school?" people asked me at parties.

"Morgan's a girl," I told them with horror.

"It's okay, Mom," Morgan whispered loudly. "I don't care!"

"You want people to think you're a boy?" I asked her, exasperated.

"Calm down, Mom," she told me, looking mortified.

What is wrong with people? Why do they say things if they aren't sure?

I started to worry that maybe Morgan was transgender. Maybe she was really a boy who had been born in a girl's body. I had written my graduate school thesis on this, and I knew what a nightmare this was.

I knocked on her door one evening and walked into her room. She was on the computer.

"Morgan, do you want to be a boy?"

"What?" she yelled, immediately agitated. "No, Mom, I don't want to be a boy. I'm a girl through and through."

"Then why do you wear boys' clothing and have such short hair? Why do you want people to think you're a boy?"

"I don't, Mom. I just like the way I look." She went back to her computer, letting me know that the conversation was over.

Morgan never drank like a *normal* person. From the time she was quite young, I caught her drinking the dregs of other people's drinks when I threw parties. No alcohol was off-limits. She drank wine, beer, scotch, tequila, vodka—anything that was open.

"Never water our alcohol down," I instructed my children. "If you want to drink something, just take it, or ask me. I don't want you pouring water into the bottles."

I thought I was a very cool mom, allowing my children to imbibe when I had people over, figuring that they wouldn't need to sneak what was already allowed. They were going to drink, I figured, so why not let them do it openly?

Mark began to notice that a lot of his alcohol was missing or watered down. He started to mark his bottles with a Sharpie, playing the detective.

"Stop it, Mark!" I told him. "My children aren't drinking your alcohol. Just chill out."

"Well, it's missing all the time," he explained. "Are you drinking it?"

"No, I'm not. Just calm down, will you?"

Before she left for college, Morgan occasionally came to meet me at one of the bars across the street from our Soho loft. I would buy her a drink, and as soon as she finished it, she wanted another. She would become very talkative and intense, impressing our neighbors with her maturity and wisdom.

"Can I get another, Mom?" she would ask me.

"Morgan, you've had enough. You've had three drinks already in forty-five minutes. I'm still drinking my first glass of wine."

The more she drank, the longer she wanted to stay, conversing with me and our bar friends. Sometimes she stayed alone after I went home.

"Mom, can I have some money to buy some sodas?" she sometimes asked me.

There was a deli down the block from us, and she walked off down the street with whatever money I gave her. Typically, she carried her purchases into her room and closed the door. We found empty beer bottles hidden in her room, and she told me they were from winter vacation, or a long-ago party. Sometimes she reeked of alcohol, and when I confronted her, she always had an explanation—it was from the night before when she had sipped some wine over dinner.

Morgan seemed insane sometimes. She slurred her words, and they didn't make sense to me.

"Are you high, Morgan?" Maybe she was taking some strange drug that made her act this way.

"No, Mom," she answered, "I don't like drugs."

One afternoon, when she was about fifteen, I dragged her down to her pediatrician's office for a drug test. *If she wasn't high, she was crazy.* I didn't see other children getting glassy-eyed and incoherent. The test came back negative. *What is wrong with her? What is going to happen to my daughter, and how can I help her?*

Morgan went through therapists like other people went through shoes. She outsmarted them, even when she was in middle school. She insisted that I buy her a bag of Doritos or potato chips and a soda, and she would enter her sessions as if they were afternoon snack time. Nobody could figure out what was wrong with her, and Morgan either refused to speak to them or they no longer wanted to work with her. There was one particular female psychologist that Morgan tortured cruelly.

"Close your eyes," Morgan told her during a session while they were coloring with thick markers. Morgan was in middle school at that time, thirteen years old.

"Can I trust you?" the therapist asked her.

"Yes," Morgan assured her before drawing all over the therapist's face. Once again, I searched for another expert to help me figure out what was wrong with her and how she could be helped.

I worried about Morgan often. She seemed to find herself in some very compromising situations, and as her mother, I was afraid that something very bad was going to happen to her. One day while I was having lunch in Soho with one of my girlfriends, my phone kept ringing with a "No Caller ID" tag. I let it go into voice mail, not wanting to appear rude. After three calls, I excused myself and went outside to see who was calling me.

"This is Detective Wiggins from the Ninth Precinct," the first message began. "I have your daughter Morgan down here. She has been arrested. Please call me back."

My heart fell into my stomach. I ran back into the restaurant and told my friend, "Morgan's been arrested! I have to go right now."

I cabbed over to the precinct. Morgan had been arrested buying ten dollars' worth of weed at the projects near Bard.

"Those projects are really dangerous," the police officer told me. "I had a murder there just about a week ago. It's no place for your daughter."

Morgan was just sixteen years old. I asked to see her, and when they took me back to the cell, she was sitting nervously, her hands behind her back. I thought she was wearing handcuffs at first, but her wrists were free.

"Are you okay?" I asked.

"I've been better..." She was shaking, and she looked so young and frightened.

"Can I take her home now?" I asked the officer.

"Nope," he told me. "She needs to be arraigned in court first."

"But she's only sixteen years old!" I told him. "You can't keep her here!"

"Yes, we can," he countered.

"Her father's an attorney. Can he come down and get her out?"

"Not today."

Morgan looked panicked. "Mom, the weed wasn't even for me," she explained. "I was buying it for two of my friends." *How did she think this was better?* I didn't believe her, but if it were true, that was even worse.

Why would she put herself at risk for some other kids?

Her dad wasn't able to get her released until the next day. My little girl had just spent a night in jail. My heart was broken. Her dad got the charges dropped, but she had still been traumatized.

She was issued a court ticket the next year for having an open bottle of beer in a brown paper bag on St. Marks

Place. The friend whom she was hanging out with ran away and escaped, but Morgan wasn't one for physical activity—even under these circumstances.

"It wasn't mine," she insisted. "I was just sitting on the curb, and the bag was next to me."

Going to college at Smith was Morgan's goal and had been since middle school. She was a very good student and tested well, but I knew that it was very competitive, and I worried that she would be crushed if she didn't get in. We toured other schools, like Vassar and Wesleyan, but her heart was set on Smith. She applied "Early Decision" and was accepted right away, so she didn't have to apply any-where else. She was ecstatic, and while her classmates stressed about applications, SATs, ACTs, and where they would be spending the next four years.

The incoming class of 2015 set up a Facebook page, and Morgan was on it constantly. Morgan was known for posting inappropriate things on Facebook for years, and her father and I were very concerned that these things would follow her for the rest of her life. Her humor was reminiscent of a young, but lesbian, Sarah Silverman. Morgan wore her sexuality on her sleeve, and everyone had to know that she was gay—it was part of what defined her.

Despite our warnings, Morgan posted often on the *Smith* page, writing some off-color things. None of them were mean, or directed at anyone specifically, but they were sarcastic and sometimes of a sexual nature. She received a letter from the dean of Admissions, stating that somebody from the incoming class was offended by Morgan's postings, and they were considering rescinding her offer to attend.

"I have to go to Smith!" Morgan cried.

"What did she tell you to do?" I asked her.

"To write her a letter of apology."

"So write it and then show it to me before you send it."

Morgan drafted a fine letter, apologizing for offending somebody, and asked for the opportunity to speak to the other young woman to set it straight. The dean replied by saying that they would be discussing it over the next several business days and would let Morgan know of their decision as soon as they had reached one. If Morgan was rescinded, she was screwed. She hadn't applied anywhere else, and the deadlines for fall admissions had already passed.

Smith came back with an astonishing no, delivering the e-mail to Morgan while she was at school, though I had asked them to wait until the end of the day. I received a call from her guidance counselor, who said that Morgan was a mess, and that I should come over to get her as soon as possible. I was in the middle of a photo shoot for work but jumped into a cab to get her.

Morgan was worse than I expected when I got to Bard. She was sitting in a fetal position in a teacher's office, a ten-dollar bill ripped into pieces on the floor under her.

"What is this?" I asked her. "You ripped money?"

"So what?" she said, not looking up.

"So what? Haven't you caused enough damage already? I work hard for my money, Morgan, and it's illegal to destroy money. Do you want to go to jail again?"

It seemed easier to focus on the money than the bigger issue. My daughter's life was falling apart, and my heart was at least as broken as hers was.

We left the building and crossed Houston Street to hail a taxi. As usual, there were none to be found. Morgan wasn't speaking at all, and I was worried that she was having a nervous breakdown or that she was suicidal.

"Snap out of this!" I finally shouted at her. "You created this mess, and now you're going to have to deal with it."

She looked at me in shock, but it worked. She began to speak, and we discussed other options—colleges overseas had later admissions deadlines, the Peace Corps, finding a job, and then reapplying. I was so angry that I wanted to sue Smith, and to put Morgan on television to let other teenagers know what had happened. She could become an advocate for cleaning up social media postings. She didn't want to do any of these things. My baby girl was broken.

Smith was unwilling to change their minds, even when I called the dean of Admissions and begged her to reconsider. The posts hadn't been that bad, and I couldn't understand how they could do this to my child. They told me that the case was closed, and Morgan could reapply the following year if she wanted to.

"But she has no other options!" I told the woman on the phone. "Admissions deadlines have all passed." I was sobbing, trying to appeal to this woman's sense of human-ity—she didn't seem to have any. I was talking to deaf ears. *Clearly this woman isn't a mother. No mom would do this to a child in this position.*

Bard ended up saving the day. The principal of Bard High School / Early College (BHSEC) phoned the president of Bard College, and he was appalled by what Smith had done. Morgan and I were asked to come into school for a meeting. Everyone had reviewed the posts on Facebook, and Bard felt that the girl who was offended by Morgan should have contacted her directly. They felt that this was a nonissue and said that Morgan should fill out an application to Bard College overnight and come up the next day for an interview.

"Morgan," the principal told her, "I've read your postings on Facebook, and you're very witty. Maybe you can find a better venue for your humor when you get to college." Morgan almost smiled for the first time in two days.

We drove up to Bard in near silence the next day.

"I'm in," she said when she walked out of the Bard admissions office. "The good news is that I can finish college in two years there, since I'll already have my associates degree when I graduate this June." BHSEC covered four years of high school in the first two years and then an associate degree over the next two.

Crisis diverted.

Two years morphed into three. Morgan was working at a school for children with autism while completing her bachelor's degree. She had come to terms with not going to Smith and was getting good grades and loving her outside work. She met a girl with a younger brother who had autism, and her interest had been strongly piqued. She seemed to have found her niche. Morgan called me in the mornings, very early. I wondered how someone so young was awake this early. In college I had made a point of never taking classes that started before 10:00 a.m. I was extremely proud of the fact that she had gone away from home and was successfully navigating a rigorous schedule.

On January 27, 2015, I got a call from Morgan at around 8:00 p.m.

"Mommy," she slurred. "I think I might have a problem."

"What kind of problem?" Morgan's life had been a mess over the winter break. She had done twelve thousand dollars' worth of damage to the house she was renting with a friend up at Bard—by failing to answer phone calls from the oil company who was trying to fill her oil tank over her winter break. The pipes had frozen and caused a big mess. Next, she totaled the brand-new car that I had gotten her.

Her explanations for these events were lame, but Morgan was not great at telling the truth, and her lies usually caught up with her.

"Promise me you won't be mad," she said.

If I wasn't mad about the house and the car, what was next?

"Just tell me."

"I've been drinking a lot," she said.

"Okay. How much is a lot?" Morgan knew that I was sober and that I went to meetings every day.

"Between fifteen and thirty-five drinks a day."

What? How is that even possible?

"What do you mean? How could you drink that many drinks?"

I had seen her have four or five, and I couldn't imagine how her little body could hold much more than that. On four she was usually glassy-eyed and a bit sloppy.

"I just do," she said.

"What are you drinking?" I was imagining the kinds of drinks I had consumed during college—rum and pineapple juice, vodka and grapefruit. *How could someone drink fifteen of those?*

"Vodka or bourbon." She sounded like she was drinking something right then.

"But fifteen to thirty-five a day? How is that possible?"

"It just is. Every day I wake up and think *I'm not going to drink today.* At work, I promise myself that I won't drink, but I find myself stopping on the way home to buy a bottle. I go home and drink until I pass out. I have to check my phone in the morning to see what time I fell asleep and hope that I haven't done anything stupid."

Oh no, she's an alcoholic...she's just like me. Obsessive thinking, the inability to stop—and she was clearly blacking out.

"I have to go, Mommy. I want to call Ali. I have to tell her. Do you think she's going to break up with me?"

Ali was Morgan's girlfriend, and they had been together for three years. They were planning to live together soon, and if Ali broke up with Morgan, I didn't know what would happen.

"Why don't you call her tomorrow?" I implored her. "We can discuss what you're going to say first."

"Gotta go, Mom. Bye."

I was panicked. I had never heard of someone drinking so much, and Morgan was not a big girl. At five-foot-four, and about one hundred and twenty pounds, I didn't see how she could consume the quantities that she had described. When I hadn't heard back from her by 9:00 p.m., I tried calling her—no answer. I texted too, but she didn't respond. *What if Ali had broken up with her? Would she actually kill herself?*

Early the next morning, I called and texted again. Her phone was still going straight to voice mail. I figured that she was at work, but why wouldn't she let me know she was okay? I left her at least a dozen messages.

Finally, I texted her housemate: *Is Morgan okay?*

Yeah, she's great, he replied immediately.

Did you see her today?

Yes. She's fine.

A close friend of mine from New York was staying with Mark and me in Delray Beach at the time, and another was arriving later that morning. I drove to the airport to get her. We went shopping to buy a few things on our way home, and while we were shopping, Morgan's landlord called me. I let the call go to voice mail, explaining to my friend how this woman was after me for the damages Morgan had caused to her house. Morgan signed a lease on a house that had no insurance coverage. A few minutes later, the woman called again, and I let it go to voice mail.

"Maybe I should listen to that message," I told my friend. "She normally doesn't call me more than once a day."

"Hi, Mallory, this is Anne, Morgan's landlord. I'm calling you about Morgan. I had to call an ambulance. I found her in sort of a catatonic state. She's on her way to the hospital—I'm following the ambulance. She was supposed to babysit today. She's okay, I think."

I left my houseguests from New York with Mark and flew to Upstate New York on the first possible flight. The airport was more than an hour away from the hospital, and I drove my rental car through ice and snow, desperate to see her. I called every expert that I knew in the field, asking them what to do. The answers were pretty much unanimous—detox, followed by inpatient treatment. Morgan had blown a 0.592 at the hospital. This was more than seven times the blood alcohol level for intoxication, which was .08. The emergency room doctor was particularly concerned by the fact that Morgan was coherent at this blood alcohol level. Most people would be dead or in a coma, and brain damage was common.

"Get me out of here!" Morgan cried when I got to the hospital. I had implored the hospital to keep her until I was able to get there, which was almost a full day later.

I hugged her. She looked fine, other than the fact that she was desperate to leave the hospital and adamant that she didn't need detox.

"I'm fine!" she insisted. "I don't need detox!"

The emergency room doctor disagreed. "She had a huge amount of alcohol in her system. I definitely recommend detox."

"I'm not going to detox!" she screamed again.

"She could have seizures," the doctor continued.

"I'm not going to have a seizure," Morgan insisted.

"How long is the detox period?" I asked the doctor.

"Four to five days."

"I'll take her to a hotel and watch her," I told him. "If anything happens, I'll call an ambulance immediately.

Morgan and I checked into a beautiful bed and breakfast in Rhinebeck. It was right near the A.A. meeting that I attended regularly whenever I visited.

"I can't go to rehab!" Morgan told me over and over. "Then I won't be able to graduate in May. I can't spend another year up here!"

"How am I going to leave you up here, knowing that you almost died?" I asked.

"I won't drink, Mommy! I promise!"

Over the next four days, we devised a plan. Morgan would finish Bard in May as long as she didn't pick up a single drop of alcohol between now and then. She would attend A.A. meetings every day and get a sponsor. I found a therapist who had offices in Rhinebeck and Manhattan, and we met with him. Morgan liked him, and he agreed to see her every week. We met with the dean of Bard, Morgan's advisor, and the head of medical services. I wanted everyone to be aware of what had happened. They told us about a 12-step meeting on campus that met every Thursday night, and Morgan committed to attending.

I took her to my A.A. meetings every morning. Luckily I found a regular meeting in Rhinebeck that I attended whenever I visited Morgan.

"Please take care of my daughter like you took care of me," I cried every day. "I live in Florida, and I can't be here to watch over her. Please help my daughter."

I was in tears every time I raised my hand and shared. The members gathered around Morgan after the first meeting, and a lovely woman who I had seen for several years offered to sponsor her. Things were falling into place. We couldn't find an IOP for Morgan near her school or her work, which upset me. I had learned a lot at my IOP.

Morgan suggested that we buy a Breathalyzer and that she would Facetime with me as many times every day and night as I asked her. We went out and bought one together. Morgan breathalyzed with me on Facetime at least twice a day until her graduation. She would turn the Breathalyzer on and let me watch the numbers. Then she would blow in and show me the results—0.00 every time. True to her word, she did not drink a sip of alcohol. She got sober in the rooms of A.A., and at the time of this writing she has over two and a half years sober.

Today, Morgan lives in Brooklyn. She has a wonderful job at a school in Manhattan for children with autism. She and Ali have been living together for over two years. She goes to meetings and is excelling in graduate school. She also works with some of her students outside school hours. Her life is sober and free—she has learned to hang out with other people and to be honest about her recovery.

Five years ago, I wanted to die. At that time, I asked Morgan if she would be okay without me, and she assured me that she would. I truly believe that if I hadn't found recovery and the A.A. program, both of us would be dead. Instead, we have wonderful times together and help others who are trying to find their way in the world.

As a child, whenever I drove my mother crazy, she would say, "I wish you a daughter just like yourself." She didn't mean it in a kind way. Well, guess what, Mom? You got your wish. And I wouldn't trade Morgan for anything in the world.

Sober House

If I Build It, Will They Come?

I moved to Delray Beach, Florida, in September 2014, after a lifetime in New York City. My youngest child, Jack, had just started his freshman year at Boston University, setting me free from the city I had wanted to escape for over twenty years. Selling my loft in Soho had netted me enough cash to open a sober house and invest even more with a money manager. Somehow I bought a house, furnished it, and got all the certifications and legalities for a sober house in order.

Everyone had an opinion.

"You're going to lose all your money," my father told me on the phone, sounding extremely sad that I was thinking of doing this.

"If it doesn't work, I can always sell the house after renovating, or rent it out," I told him.

"Sounds like a great idea," my husband and daughter told me.

"Why don't you just take some time off and relax?" my father persisted.

"I don't really understand it," my accountant said, "but it sounds interesting. There isn't too much downside since the house is a solid asset."

I was working part-time as a group facilitator at a rehab in West Palm Beach. I was taking golf lessons, playing tennis, and practicing yoga. I had been walking the beach every morning for several months, planning things out, deciding on a name. The meetings with all kinds of people were endless—making sure I was doing things properly, ethically, legally. Opening a sober house was serious business, and I had all intentions of doing things properly. I knew I was doing this for the right reasons, and I didn't want to screw anything up.

I had invested my little trust fund wisely in real estate, and the money I made from the first house I sold allowed me to buy a more expensive one next, and then a third and fourth. I doubled or tripled my money every time. So by the time I packed up my life in New York, I had a little nest egg. My dream of opening a sober house was foremost in my mind, and I hoped that I would finally be able to dedicate myself full-time to helping others. My addiction had nearly killed me, and I wanted to do the work that I believed I was born to do.

At night I lay in bed until midnight or later with my laptop on my legs, ordering furniture online, writing e-mails to carpenters and handymen, choosing paint colors, pricing out vendors. My husband was commuting back and forth between Manhattan and Delray Beach, giving me a lot of uninterrupted time to work on everything from selecting a color palette to filling out endless forms for the city, the state, the country.

In late December 2014, I visited the house after work and couldn't believe what I saw: it was ready. Women could really move in. There was only one problem—nobody knew it existed.

I knew about marketing because I had worked in the field for eighteen years. I needed to work on my brand, build a website, design a logo, plan and print business cards. I had to hit the road and tell people I was finally here—I needed to quit my job.

I gave two weeks' notice the next morning, thinking that my supervisors were going to be thrilled about my new venture. They loved having me work there, so surely they would want their patients to come and live in my home when they finished treatment there, right? There was a real shortage of good women's sober homes. I was told that there were more than ten men's houses for every women's house. Why? "Because women are hormonal, gossipy, and unkind to each other," I was told. Well, I loved women and I am a woman, so I was up for the challenge!

"You can't take patients from here," my direct boss told me when I shared my exciting news. "It's a conflict of interest."

"I thought you would want to send your patients to a safe place where you know the owner."

"We need to check with corporate," she continued in a voice that made it clear that she would not be taking the time to do so.

That was not the reaction I had expected. If *they* didn't want to refer to me, then who would? I worried about this on my drive home that day. Why wouldn't they want their departing women to be with someone they already knew and trusted? Maybe nobody would ever come. What had I done?

Was she jealous that I was opening my own business? Too busy to make a phone call? Upset that I was giving notice?

Calm down, I told myself. *You can always sell the house if nobody moves in.*

I tried to manage my costs and do certain things on the cheap. I designed a logo online with a supercool graphic designer from California. With that I created my own business card. The website would be more difficult, and I spoke to a few agencies who had built similar sites, got quotes, and checked out their portfolios. I found a small husband-and-wife operation somewhere in Florida and began working with them via phone and e-mail. It took a lot of dialogue and tweaking, but we finally got it right.

The brochures came next, and the web agency also worked on this, as I wanted a cohesive brand image. It had to look clean, sunny, and cheerful. That was the whole feel that I was striving for. When it came to attorneys, certification, and insurance, I went all out, hiring the very best resources in the field.

I created a sunny, comfortable home. My marketing materials followed, and they had to portray the same feeling as the house did. The first set of brochures was a complete disaster, but I used them at first anyway as I needed something to hand out when I went to speak to potential referral sources. I scheduled meetings at rehabs and tried to get in front of as many people as I could to share my vision. I cringed every time someone complimented my poorly designed, printed, and folded brochures, reassuring them that the new and improved version was on its way.

"We love your vision," the first rehab I visited and marketed to told me after I poured my heart and soul out to more than a dozen clinicians and discharge planners. "But we don't refer to sober houses that have been in business for less than two years." *Two years?* I cringed inside. *In two years, I could be out of business if nobody referred to me.*

I was two years sober. I had never worked at a sober house. I had never lived in a sober house. Was anybody going to believe in me?

I honestly didn't know how all this happened. I came up with the name on the beach one morning during one of my brainstorming walks. I was looking for something feminine, beachy, involving nature and animals. Butterflies? Lily pads? My mom had died from alcoholism, and she collected frogs. What about the Lily Pad?

"Taken," my lawyers informed me.

"The Frog Pad then," I suggested. I loved frogs and always have. I had owned two as pets when I was a little girl. I had trudged through swamps at sleepaway camp as a child, catching frogs of all sizes, organizing frog races with my friends.

"The Frog Pad" it was. Name not taken. We *jumped* on it.

The first house that my real estate broker showed me had a canal running behind it. The canal was filled with green plants. "What are those?" I asked the owner.

"Lily pads," he replied.

"Are there a lot of frogs here?" I asked, looking at my real estate broker with a little smile.

"Yes, there are. And turtles, and fish and birds."

I was sold.

The house had six bedrooms, four bathrooms, a large swimming pool, an outdoor shower, a hammock, and a meditation beach. There were multiple washer/dryers, two kitchens, and lots of closets. Everything was here except the residents.

Other sober homeowners told me they hadn't gotten their first resident for five months, even eight months. I brought people over for tours, spoke of my vision for a house for women that was sober, safe, fun, loving. A place where women could transition after rehab, planting their feet in 12-step meetings and recovery, which I found really worked for ongoing sobriety. I wanted to share the things that had helped me in my early recovery, like yoga and guided meditation. My house would allow the women to build friendships with other women in recovery, and they would be together during difficult holidays and special occasions without picking up a drink or a drug. I added more—Thai massage, reflexology, career counseling, and nutrition. I would bring in an array of sober women who offered this menu of services and introduce them to my residents. The ladies who lived with me would see that these women in recovery were beautiful inside and out, that they were sober and their lives were filled with meaning and purpose.

My phone rang at about seven one morning about three weeks after the house was complete.

"Hey, Mallory," a very slurred voice began. "It's Kerri."

"Good morning. How are you doing?" This wasn't the first time she had called me drunk, but it was the earliest.

I met Kerri at an A.A. meeting in Delray Beach about six months earlier. She was anxious to leave her posh rehab and return home to Long Island to her husband and daughters. She was not ready to admit complete defeat, to reach out to the sober women I had tried to connect her with at home. She did not go to the A.A. meetings I had recommended or to an IOP. She had been attracted to my upscale yoga clothes and my Chanel handbag. And now she was drunk. Very drunk. At seven in the morning.

"I need your help," she continued. "I need to move into the Frog House."

I was surprised that she even knew that I had a house, even if she had the name jumbled. I guessed that Facebook was responsible. I didn't even know that we were friends on Facebook. I hadn't thought of her in months.

"Nobody's here yet," I told her. "You would be the only one."

"That's perfect," she replied. "I'm going to book a flight now."

"For when?"

"I'll be there today."

I told her the price, and she did not even balk.

"My husband will pay with a credit card," she told me.

"Don't drink anymore," I warned her. "If you do, I'm not going to be able to put you in the house."

"I won't," she promised.

About five hours later, I was waiting at Palm Beach International to pick her up. Everyone got off the plane except her. I waited about fifteen minutes and then called her.

"Where are you?" she asked me in an entitled voice.

"I'm waiting at Arrivals," I informed her.

"I've been here for a long time," she told me, still sounding miffed.

Apparently she had been waiting for me at the gate, where nobody was allowed unless they were boarding a flight themselves. She finally made her way to Arrivals, and she could barely walk down to the baggage claim area with me. She was wearing workout clothes and sneakers, but even in flats she could not keep her balance. She was so thin that I thought an eating disorder had joined her alcoholism.

"Which bag is yours?" I asked her when we got to the carousel. Almost every bag had already been claimed while she had waited at the gate. She had no idea. I had to call her husband to identify it.

"So...I guess you drank on the plane," I confirmed as we walked to get my car in the parking garage.

"I just had half a glass of wine," she said, looking at me with innocent brown eyes. She looked awful—messy in her wrinkled workout garb, her dark hair trailing out of her usually tidy ponytail.

More like a bottle of wine, I thought to myself as I made sure she buckled herself in.

"I'm bringing you to my house to sleep it off," I told her. She wasn't sober, so she couldn't stay at the sober house, even if she was the only one there.

"I want to go to the Four Seasons," she stated, looking and sounding like a spoiled child.

The Four Seasons is in Palm Beach, and Kerri had promised to accompany me to the 7:00 a.m. A.A. meeting in Delray Beach where we had met months earlier. She was going to pick up a white chip, which signifies that she is ready to surrender herself to the program and stop drinking.

"It's way too far, Kelly. I'm not driving you there and then picking you up at the crack of dawn for the meeting."

"Then I'll stay at the Seagate," she continued. "I want a nice piece of fish and a glass of wine tonight. I'll start fresh tomorrow."

I called her husband again.

"I am not paying for a hotel!" he insisted. "Please keep her at your house tonight."

After sulking a bit, Kerri agreed to stay at my house, but she stumbled across the street to the Seagate Hotel for her piece of fish and her (hopefully) last glass of wine. When she wasn't home two hours later, I went out to look for her and found her sitting on the side of the street. She was lost, though my home was only half a block away. She was in a good mood now and ready to go to sleep.

The fun had just begun. I was officially in business.

Getting In

It was around nine on a Thursday night, and I was in bed with Mark, watching an episode of *Ray Donovan*. My phone rang, and I saw a Tennessee number on the screen.

"I'm going to get this," I said. "Could be business."

Mark paused the show, making only a soft sigh. We loved watching our shows together, but business always came first for both of us.

"Hello?"

"Is this The Frog Pad?" a woman with a Southern accent asked.

"Yes, it is. I'm Mallory... I'm the owner."

"My daughter is at treatment in Florida right now. She has never gone to sober living out of state before, but I think she needs it this time."

"What's your name?" I asked her, trying to slow her down a bit.

"Oh, I'm Jillian," she said with a twang.

"And what's your daughter's name?"

"Audrey. I named her after Audrey Hepburn. Such a beautiful actress she was."

"How old is Audrey?"

"She's twenty-five, and I'm terrified that she's going to die. I can't take this anymore. She's my whole life."

"Well, she's safe right now if she's in treatment, right?"

"Yes, but this is her tenth treatment in the past eight years. This damn heroin is going to kill my little girl." Jillian's voice was getting louder, and she sounded a bit hysterical.

"Her father is an addict too, and he's a complete loser. He's in prison again, and she got this from him. I've never done drugs in my life."

"Addiction is a disease. It's no different than having cancer, or diabetes. Many addicts and alcoholics have other affected family members, but not everyone does."

"I know that. She has been in treatment ten times already. I go to Al-Anon almost every day. I have an Al-Anon sponsor."

"That's great, so I'm sure you know that addiction is also an allergy of the body and an obsession of the mind. People who are allergic to peanuts don't eat peanut butter sandwiches, but addicts keep trying to figure out a way to drink or do drugs safely. But once we have truly crossed into addiction we will always end up in the same mess again eventually. And with opiates, unfortunately, so many people are crossing that line younger and younger."

"I've been looking at your website, and I want Audrey to come to your house. It's different than any house I've ever seen before, and the houses here in Memphis are just terrible flophouses."

We discussed where Audrey was currently at treatment and when she would be leaving. She told me Audrey's history and where else she had been in treatment, both inpatient and outpatient, and which sober houses she had lived in previously. She had been to some very good treatment centers, but the sober houses had definitely been lacking.

"Staying sober in rehab is pretty easy," I told Jillian, "especially when our parents are financially responsible for us. It's what happens when we leave treatment that will truly determine whether or not we stay sober."

"Your houses are so beautiful," she told me. "And I love that you offer yoga. She never exercises, and she has gotten so lazy. Her eating habits are terrible. She was such a beautiful young girl until this heroin got her."

"Going to treatment ten times is not necessarily the best way to get sober. I went to an IOP in New York for thirty-two days, and I have been sober since my first day there. Staying sober is a choice—and working a 12-step program is the way we stay sober."

"Audrey does so well in treatment, but every time she gets out, she moves back in with me and she ends up using again. I drug test her and everything, but she keeps doctor shopping and getting pills. I just can't take this anymore!" Jillian sounded like she was crying now.

"My daughter got sober at twenty, and she never even went to treatment," I told her. "I took her to A.A. near her college, and she got a sponsor, went to meetings, and has been sober even since. This program really works if you work it."

"The meetings in Tennessee are terrible. Everybody is so redneck and down and out. There's nobody here that my Audrey can relate to."

"I go to meetings everywhere," I said, "and I always hear the message. We are all the same in recovery, and we need to learn to relate to others, rather than to compare or judge them. The disease does not discriminate. It doesn't matter if we're rich or poor, young or old. People of every race and religion have stayed sober, working this beautiful program. At my sober house we have a very big focus on 12-step meetings, and every woman has to get a sponsor."

"My Audrey is so smart. She wants to be a lawyer. She went to college."

"She can be anything she wants to be if she just gets sober and works a program every day. I have seen miracles."

We discussed price, and I asked Jillian to have Audrey and her therapist at treatment call me to schedule a phone interview.

"I run a very loving house," I said. "A lot of sober houses are militant with their residents, and very punishing. I don't believe in that. I believe that if we aren't happy in our recovery, we will end up using again. We are all so broken when we come in—like birds with a broken wing. In my houses, I love all of my women until they can love themselves. There is no 'mean girls' behavior allowed. Everyone must treat one another with kindness and acceptance. I have had as many women leave my house because they couldn't be kind as those who have been asked to leave due to a relapse."

"Oh, that's just what Audrey needs!" Jillian exclaimed. "I'm the only person who has ever loved her. She needs someone else to love her too. She and I only have each other."

I could tell that Jillian was petrified and also that she was extremely codependent. This could make for a very difficult recovery for the child. The parents would just keep picking up the pieces every time their daughter screwed up, and sometimes they would even sabotage their recovery by bringing them home before they were ready.

"Will Audrey be attending an IOP when she gets to sober living?"

"Yes, absolutely."

"Great. I will discuss a few options with her discharge planner when I hear from them."

It was 10:30 p.m. when we got off the phone. It was always important not to rush these calls, and to be very clear with our requirements, and to get as much history as possible. The families had to know that their loved ones would be safe and cared for. Mark was fast asleep, our dogs curled up beside him. *Ray Donovan* would need to resume on another night.

Audrey and her discharge planner called me that Monday, and she fit all our criteria. She was coming from inpatient treatment, she wanted to be sober, and she understood all our rules and requirements.

"I love my mother so much," Audrey told me on the phone, "but every time I go back home I end up relapsing. It has been happening for almost eight years already. I'm not blaming her, but I definitely feel like I need a change, and that's why I came to Florida this time. It's the first time I left Tennessee for treatment. I know I can't go back there yet."

I picked Audrey up from treatment several weeks later. She was very shy on the ride to Delray Beach, and I worked hard to draw her out and put her at ease.

"How did you end up shooting heroin?" I asked.

"I met a guy at treatment a few years ago, and we fell in love. He was a lot older than me, and he shot me up from behind the first time. I didn't even know he was doing it."

"You mean he tricked you into doing it?"

"Yep, I would have never done heroin. I was strictly pills and alcohol. The minute it happened though, I loved it. I was shooting myself up within days."

"You're going to love the other women at the houses," I promised her. "I'll pick you up in the morning tomorrow and take you to a women's meeting at Crossroads." (Crossroads is a meeting clubhouse in Delray Beach with 12-step meetings morning, noon, and night.) "It's a good place to look for a sponsor because there are a lot of women with long-term sobriety there who work solid programs."

"When can I go food shopping?" she asked me as we neared the house. "I haven't had a healthy meal in almost three months."

"I'll take you to Publix right after we do your intake," I promised her. She was starving after her intake, so I treated her to lunch at a local diner before taking her to the supermarket. She ordered a giant sub, french fries, and a large Coke.

"I haven't had a Coke in months," she told me happily, after refilling her large cup a second time. "I'm in heaven." She laughed for the first time, and I saw a beautiful light in her eyes. *She's going to be okay.*

"You're IOP is picking you up tomorrow morning at eleven for an intake interview, so you can just unpack today and tonight and get to know some of the other residents. They're all so excited to meet you."

Welcome, Audrey!

Can't wait to meet you tonight.

Let's have dinner together later.

Hi. I'm your roommate. See you soon.

These were some of the responses that started streaming into Audrey's phone as soon as I sent out a new group text announcing her arrival. We communicated via group text often.

"Wow!" she laughed. "Everyone seems so nice and friendly. I've never had this at a sober house before."

"We're a big sober family—sisters, mothers, daughters, friends. It's a beautiful fellowship."

"I'm so excited! I can't wait to call my mom and tell her all about it."

You are truly an angel from heaven, Jillian wrote to me late that night in a text message. *I haven't heard Aud this happy in the past eight years. She feels like you are really going to be her sober mother. She loves the house, and the other women are making her feel so welcome.*

I told you I would love her and take care of her. She is adorable.

Thank you, dear woman, for what you do. I can sleep soundly tonight, knowing that my Audrey is safe and happy.

My work was not always easy, but words like these reminded me of why I was here. Becoming an addict and then finding recovery had given me an entirely new life. I had meaning and purpose now. My life and work were truly entwined for the first time.

Love you, sweet girl, I texted to Audrey. *Sweet dreams tonight.*

Love you too.

Arriving Sober, or Not

Addiction is very patient. People can stay sober while at inpatient rehabs for long periods of time, where it is virtually impossible for them to drink or get high. As soon as they leave, though, many find themselves drinking or using again, even when they had no intention or desire to do so.

Catherine was at a rehab in Florida when her discharge planner called me. "I have a woman who needs a sober living home. She's discharging next Sunday, but she needs to go home for two weeks to clear up some legal issues before she comes to you."

"That's a really bad idea. She should move in first and then go home to clear things up."

"She has a deadline, and she needs to complete some drunk driving classes by the end of the month." Catherine lived two hours away from my house, so she couldn't drive back and forth. Her license had been suspended anyway for driving under the influence (DUI).

213

Catherine's mother called me. "Catherine has to complete these courses," she informed me. "She'll be fine."

"Will she be staying with you while she's there?"

"No," her mother said. "I'm going to put her in a motel. I'm not speaking to her again until she has a year sober. I've been dealing with her addiction for over twenty years, and I can't handle it. I'm eighty-one years old."

A lot of parents and families felt this way. They were disappointed so many times by the addicts and alcoholics in their lives that they had learned to detach. They had often double mortgaged their homes and cashed in their 401Ks in order to help their sick family member, and at some point many of them were finished being hurt and deceived. Regardless of their inherent love for their daughters (or sisters, granddaughters, wives, mothers), at some point they were being impacted so negatively that they had to walk away.

"I'm afraid that she'll relapse if she doesn't come here right away," I told her mother. "It's very important for her to have accountability when she leaves treatment."

"She is not going to relapse," her mother promised me. "She has eleven courses to complete, and she will be going to A.A. meetings every day."'

Her mother sent the deposit and the rent check, and I held a bed for Catherine. She was to arrive two weeks after her discharge.

The night before Catherine was expected to arrive at The Frog Pad, I received a phone call from her mother.

"Mallory, there's been a little glitch. Catherine is in jail, but she's fine."

The words "jail" and "fine" did not mesh for me. "What happened?"

"She drank a wine cooler, so she turned herself in. She called me, and I took her to the jailhouse. They are ready to release her whenever you write a letter to the deputy and let him know that she is being released to your sober house."

I figured that she could dry out in jail, and by the time she arrived a few days later, she would be ready to start anew. Her mother gave me the details for the deputy, and I composed and e-mailed the letter to him before I went to sleep that night.

The next day, I was doing errands for the sober house when my phone rang.

"Is this Mallory Neuberger?" a man's deep, confident voice inquired.

"Yes, it is."

"This is Deputy Douglas. I have Catherine with me, and we're looking for your house."

Oh no, this is not going to be good.

"Where are you exactly?"

He told me he was a block away from the house.

"Wait out front," I said. "I'll be there in ten minutes."

There was little that I liked less than having a police car in front of my sober house. I worked very hard to keep our address off the internet, and I didn't need nosy neighbors coming around to see what was happening. Luckily the lights on his car weren't flashing when I pulled up.

Catherine got out of the car, and she was not a pretty sight. She was tall and emaciated. Her dark eyes were bulging out of her pale face, and she was shaking visibly.

"Hi, Catherine," I said, putting my arms around her and pulling her into a loose hug. "Welcome."

"I really need a cigarette," she said, her eyes darting around wildly.

"Where are her things?" I asked the good-looking deputy.

"She didn't have anything when she came in."

No handbag. No cigarettes. No money. No phone. No clothing.

The deputy left, driving off into the beautiful day, leaving me with a nervous and clearly traumatized woman.

"Do you have a cigarette?" she asked me again.

"No, I don't, and you need to come inside and fill out your paperwork."

As we filled out her intake forms, it became clear to me that she was not okay. I only interviewed her on the telephone, so I hadn't seen her before, but she was agitated and seemed high. I showed her how we breathalyzed our residents every day, and she had not been drinking.

"What exactly did you drink?" I asked. "Your mom said it was just one wine cooler."

"Oh, no. I was drinking and using the whole time. I fell down in the lobby of the motel, and some guy picked me up and had to take me to my room."

Many of my residents did not tell their families the whole truth. Like the addicts they were, they shared only what they needed to and protected the gory details.

I gave Catherine a UA (urine analysis). She peed in front of me, and then I dipped the twelve-panel drug screen into the small plastic cup of urine. We stood together, waiting for the results to show up. She was positive for cocaine and benzos (short for benzodiazepines, which included Xanax, Klonopin, and Valium).

"Catherine, you're testing positive for benzos and cocaine. You can't stay here. You're going to have to go back to detox."

I called the treatment center that she had been discharged from over a week earlier and asked them if they could take her back for detox. An hour later we were on our way back.

"This is why I ask that my residents come to me directly from treatment." I asked, "How many of your classes and meetings did you actually make it to?"

"One class, no meetings."

She had been on a drinking-and-drugging binge since the day after she left treatment. Now she would spend ten to twelve days in detox before she could come back to my house. She would have to attend a minimum of two months in an outpatient program four days a week, meet individually with a therapist, and attend meetings every single day for ninety days.

I am pleased to say that Catherine returned directly to The Frog Pad when she was released from detox. She successfully completed her outpatient program, attended meetings daily for a year, got a sponsor, and worked the 12-steps; then she began working again and returned to her hometown on her one-year anniversary, where her mother was back in her life. Catherine is working a 12-step program at home and continues to work. She remains clean and sober.

Bridget was another resident who did not come to sober living directly after finishing treatment. She was nineteen years old and had returned to her parents' home in Georgia a couple of weeks before they called me. Bridget sounded adorable on the phone, and she said that she felt she needed the structure and accountability of a sober house. She feared that she would relapse if she remained at home. She was an IV heroin user, and her parents were petrified that their daughter was going to die if she relapsed.

After I conducted a phone interview, her parents were on board and said they would be driving down to Delray Beach with Bridget the following weekend and would leave the car for their daughter to drive. They had heard of my house from one of my current residents—a young woman named Allison, who was a total disaster. Bridget and Allison met at treatment and had become fast friends. Allison was released earlier than Bridget and had been living at my house for about a month.

Allison hated me and hated my house. The only reason she was there was because she was in serious legal trouble and would have been in jail if she hadn't agreed to treatment and sober living. Allison was very vocal about the fact that she was only eighteen years old and was not done drinking or taking drugs. She was just staying sober for as long as she had to before she could go home to Texas and get a new car again. She was spoiled and whiny, and I was constantly meeting with her to discuss her bad attitude.

"Just fake it until you make it," I kept telling her. "Maybe you'll actually start to like being sober if you keep doing it and going to meetings."

"I'm not going to like it," she insisted, looking at me with her angry blue eyes. She could have been a pretty girl, but her lack of interest in her appearance, coupled with her bad attitude, made her very unattractive.

"Why don't you just leave if you hate it so much?" I asked her.

"I can't or I would. My parents won't support me any more if I leave."

"Well, you're not staying here unless you're kind, respectful, and compliant."

I couldn't kick her out because she did the bare minimum that was required. She attended IOP, went to 12-step meetings almost every day, completed her chores, and kept her room neat. I was just hoping that some of the good things that were happening for her housemates would rub off on her. Her parents couldn't handle her anymore and wanted her to stay with me for a minimum of six months.

"Bridget's going to be on a very strict car allowance," I told her parents. "She won't be allowed to drive at all until she has been with us for at least a week, and we will revisit it then, and assess how she's doing." They all agreed to these terms and said they would sign Bridget up for a good nearby IOP.

Allison was thrilled that Bridget was coming. She hadn't connected with any of the other residents in the house and tended to stay in her room listening to music on her headphones or using her laptop. Apparently, the plan for Bridget to come to Florida to room with Allison had been brewing since Bridget got out of treatment. Allison's attitude started to get better as soon as she learned that Bridget was definitely moving in.

"Bridget's my best friend," Allison told me. "I'm so happy she's coming!" The corners of her lips almost turned up, suggesting that there might actually be a smile hidden somewhere inside her tough-girl exterior.

Both sets of parents felt that the girls were good influences on each other, so I arranged for them to share a room. It was a big, beautiful room, with a private bathroom that had a soaking tub, a big European shower, double sinks, and a walk-in closet the size of a small studio apartment in Manhattan. The girls were excited that they were about to be reunited, and I hoped that Bridget would be a positive influence on Allison's lukewarm recovery.

Bridget arrived with her ultraconservative parents on a Sunday afternoon. They had been driving for two days and stayed in motels along the way. Bridget was adorable, with long almost-black hair. She had long dark eyelashes and big green eyes. She was dressed like a stripper, in short shorts and a sleeveless blouse tied just above her belly button and unbuttoned almost down to her belly button. After completing her paperwork, Bridget and Allison went into their room and closed the door. Her parents headed off to the airport, looking exhausted enough to fall asleep in the Uber.

When I arrived at the house the next morning to check on them, one of the other residents told me that Bridget and Allison had snuck out of the house after curfew the night before. They left at about 1:00 a.m. and hadn't returned until around 7:00 a.m. I was furious. My house manager Betsy was there doing bed and chore checks as she did every morning and distributing meds. I asked her to come into Allison and Bridget's room with me.

"Time to pee, girls," I announced as I barged into their room. Both of them were fast asleep, though it was 9:30 a.m. and the house called for 9:00 a.m. wake up. "Wake up!"

Despite their youth, both of them looked exhausted.

"You first," I told Bridget, escorting her into the bathroom with the pee cup. She urinated and handed me the cup.

"Your turn," I told Allison.

I placed the cups on the vanity and dipped the twelve-panel screens in for ten seconds and then sealed them up and placed them on a paper towel, waiting for the results, which could take as long as five minutes to register. Allison was clean, but Bridget was positive for opiates.

I closed the bedroom door so we had complete privacy. A relapse was always upsetting in a sober house, and I didn't want the other women to get upset. I would speak to them privately once I had things taken care of.

"Sit on your beds," I told both girls. My house manager Betsy and I started searching their room, beginning with their handbags and nightstands. Within minutes, I found a handful of plastic syringes in Bridget's bag. She admitted that she had been shooting up at rest stops all the way from Texas, her parents completely oblivious.

"How dare you bring these into my sober house!" I said. "You are out! Pack your bags right now. I'm calling your parents."

"And you," I said to Allison, "snuck out after curfew last night, so we need to discuss the consequences of your actions as soon as I'm done dealing with Bridget."

"If she's leaving, then I'm leaving with her," Allison said, glaring at me with defiance.

"Well, let's see what your parents have to say about that."

Both girls started packing up their belongings. They had so much stuff that it looked like they were packing up a small boutique. Betsy was overseeing their packing while I called both sets of parents to explain what was happening. Allison's father was furious, because she was on probation, and he didn't want her leaving the state of Florida or getting in any more trouble. If she went back to Illinois, she could be locked up.

"I'm not paying for anything!" he yelled. "She has to stay at your house and follow your rules!"

I put Allison on the phone with him.

"I am *not* staying here without Bridget!" she screamed. "She came here to be with me, and I'm not leaving her. I didn't take drugs—only she did!"

Bridget's parents were mortified and sounded exhausted and completely beaten down when I reached them.

"What are our options?" they asked.

"Well, she can't stay here right now. I can put her in a detox, or I can take her to a hotel. I would take her cash and credit cards and let her sleep it off for a few days until we figure our next steps."

"Give me my car!" Bridget started screaming. "Give me my car keys! I need to get out of here right now!"

"She's demanding that I give her the car," I told her parents.

"Do not give her the car under any circumstances," her father said. "That car is in my wife's name, and if Bridget takes it, I will report it stolen."

Betsy ran over to me and gestured that she needed to tell me something urgently. I put my hand over the phone. "They're saying they're going to burn the house down!" she said. "What should we do?"

"Girls, let's get going," I told them. "I need to get Bridget off property immediately."

"I'm not getting in your car," Allison announced. "I'll call an Uber."

The two girls started dragging their bags out to the front curb, which was completely against my policy of never creating a scene in the neighborhood. Within minutes the length of the sidewalk was covered with suitcases, pillows, stuffed animals, groceries, and cases of soda. It looked like a yard sale.

"I'm leaving," Betsy said. "I can't handle this." She walked out through the garage.

"What do you mean you're leaving?" I called out to her back as she was rushing out the door.

"I have something to do."

She was gone—never to return. I received an e-mail from her the next day, telling me that she was resigning because she couldn't handle the pressure of the job. Betsy was the second house manager I had employed within a six-month period who had been unable to handle the daily pressures of working in a sober house. *Well, it is my house. I can't walk away when things get tough.*

Bridget's father reserved an oceanfront room for the girls at a posh hotel in Boca Raton. He paid for three nights. I could not believe it, and I told both sets of parents that I thought this was a very bad idea. Both girls had cash and credit cards and refused to give them to me.

Allison was arrested for disorderly conduct and public intoxication late that night. She was high on flakka—a terrible synthetic drug that recently had a slew of people jumping off bridges and pulling their clothes off in public. Her mug shot was on the internet. She looked even nastier and more defiant than I had ever seen her. Luckily for her, flakka was not considered an illegal substance. Her father retained a very expensive attorney for her. She was released from jail and escorted to the airport by the attorney, who flew her back to Illinois, the place her parents had said she could not come back to.

Bridget remained at the hotel, and her dad kept calling me and asking me to go over and give her cash.

"She had almost two hundred dollars when she left here," I told him. "What does she need cash for?"

"She says she's hungry and that she needs cigarettes," he said.

"They had tons of food," I told him. "She wants cash for heroin."

"No, she doesn't. She says she's starving."

"How much do you want me to bring her?"

"Three hundred dollars should be good," he said.

"Are you serious?" I was in disbelief at the denial and enabling that many of these parents exhibited time and time again. "She could die with three hundred dollars' worth of heroin very easily. People down here are dying from a fraction of that amount. Why don't you let me take her to the supermarket, and I'll buy her food and cigarettes?"

"She wants to go herself," he said.

I went to the hotel, with two hundred dollars in cash— the amount I had talked her father down to. When Bridget came downstairs to my car, she looked like a different person from the girl who had come to my sober house just two days earlier. Her pupils were so big that her eyes looked almost black, her makeup was smudged all around them, and her stomach was bloated and hanging over a pair of boxer shorts. She was clearly high and barely able to grab the money from me and stumble back into the hotel.

It was a beautiful sunny day. The sky was bright blue, and the air was clean and fresh. I could hear the waves outside as I drove away with my convertible top down. Bridget was locked inside the door of what was probably a dark and filthy hotel room, shooting heroin by herself, while the beautiful world went on outside. I knew, because I had been there.

Little Nightmares, Little Miracles

Working with women in early recovery is a challenge at any age, but when they are super young, there is a whole different set of issues to deal with. For one thing, it's often difficult for someone who is very young to accept that she won't be able to do something for the rest of her life. I have had drug addicts tell me that they can't imagine not drinking forever. One woman that I worked with in a rehab in South Florida, prior to opening my sober houses, was especially stuck on this.

"I'm probably going to want to drink champagne at my son's wedding," she said during a process group.

I looked at the woman. She didn't seem to be any older than twenty-five. She wore the heroin badge of honor that so many of my patients came in with these days—the "I shot heroin, so I'm super cool" attitude—you're *just* an alcoholic, or a pill popper, or whatever.

"When is your son getting married?" I asked.

"I don't have a son yet," she said. There were a few laughs from the other patients in the room.

"Why don't you just worry about today?" I suggested.

"Never" is a very long time, especially to addicts.

Some of the young women who have lived at my sober houses have been extremely motivated. I had a twenty-year-old move in, a stripper from Las Vegas named Autumn. She was a heroin addict and the mother of a very young baby girl, and she felt that she had only one chance at recovering. Her family had saved up enough money to fly her to Florida, send her to a PHP (this was a partial hospitalization program that ran six days a week for five hours a day) for thirty days, and to live in a sober house. She truly wanted her daughter back (the baby was currently living with her father, who was still in active addiction), and she knew that she had to get sober in order to get her baby back.

I was nervous when I picked Autumn up at Fort Lauderdale airport. She was my second resident, and I wasn't sure what to expect of a heroin addict–stripper from Las Vegas. I was picturing a hard-looking woman to walk off the plane—silicone breasts, high heels, false eyelashes, skintight jeans. Autumn was none of these things. She walked into the waiting area looking as scared as I felt. She was a tiny, little thing, with dark Hispanic-looking skin and jet-black hair tied back in a messy ponytail. She was wearing jeans, a hoodie, and flat shoes. She was a little bit chubby and did not look like a stripper at all. Her face was almost makeup-free, and she was carrying a teddy bear and a pillow. She looked petrified. She had never been out of the state of Nevada or taken an airplane before.

"Are you nervous?" I asked as we waited for her suitcase.

"Yes, very," she admitted.

I put my arms around her and gave her a big hug.

"We'll take care of you," I promised her. "Addiction sucks, and you don't have to live this way anymore."

"I have to get better," she said, looking at me with her dark almond-shaped eyes. I saw pain there—things I didn't even want to know about. They were the eyes of a much-older woman, and tears welled up in them as I hugged her.

"You picked a good time to come," I said, smiling at her. "It's in the low eighties and sunny every day. We have a beautiful pool and a meditation beach. We're going to help you heal."

Autumn would often show us pictures of her baby girl. Her name was Sandy, and she looked nothing like Autumn. She was fair skinned, with red hair, clearly her father's daughter in the looks department. It was apparent that Autumn was completely in love with this little person who had been the accident of an affair with the man who had introduced Autumn to heroin, shooting her up for the very first time, and for months and months afterward.

Autumn met him at the club where she stripped. She had always earned a lot of money, and the money had paid for both her and her boyfriend to get high for the past year. He didn't work at all, keeping busy scoring drugs and shooting them both up. He was abusive as time went on, demanding that Autumn work more hours and bring home greater amounts of money. When he didn't like what she came home with, he would slap her around and verbally abuse her.

You wouldn't have known that Autumn was a highly paid stripper to look at her. Besides being chunky, she was not very sexy. She continued to gain weight during the month that she stayed with us. She ate lots of mac and cheese and potato chips. She loved candy and would down a complete jar of it every time I brought some over. She had a baby, but she really was still a child herself in many ways, comforting herself with childish foods and cuddling with her teddy bear on the living room couch when she watched TV.

Autumn was a complete pleasure to work with. She did everything that was expected of her. She attended treatment six days a week, went to A.A. or NA meetings every day, and complied with all the house rules. She remained sober and worked very hard to learn all that she could.

As more women moved in, Autumn quickly became the house favorite. Everyone was touched by the pictures of her little baby and of Autumn's intense desire to get her daughter back.

At night we played club music and tried to get her to dance for us. "Come on, Autumn!" I coaxed, dancing around the kitchen. "Show us some of your moves." She watched us white girls dance badly, but she was not willing to show us her stuff.

One night we finally got her to twerk for us. She wagged her rounded butt better than the other women could, but I still couldn't envision her stripping on a stage.

"What are you going to do when you get back to Vegas?" I asked her one day as I was driving her to an NA meeting.

"I'm going back to the club."

"Really? Isn't that going to be triggering for you?" I asked, concerned that people, places, and things would take her back to her old ways.

"It's the only way I can afford to support my daughter and pay my family back," she explained. Stripping was all she had ever known. She had graduated high school and gone right to the clubs.

"Aren't you worried about being around the same people, drinking and drugging all the time?"

"A little," she admitted, "but I've already looked up NA and A.A. meetings near me, and I'm going to start going to them as soon as I get home. I'll bring Sandy with me."

Thirty days after I picked her up at the airport, I dropped her back off. She flew back to Las Vegas and was reunited with her daughter. She has been sober ever since. I watch her progress on Facebook from time to time. She has Sandy full-time now, and she posts pictures of them together, laughing and snuggling. Sandy's hair has darkened now, and she resembles her mother more and more. Autumn has slimmed down, and she looks happy and beautiful. Several months ago she posted that she had been sober for two years.

And then there are the girls who are sent away by their families—*Intervention* style. They are screwing up at college or even in high school, partying too much, getting DUIs or just miserable grades.

Ruby was a cute little nineteen-year-old with a history of running away and acting out with men and women sexually. When I spoke to her parents on the phone, they shared their terrible fears, and I assured them that my house was safe and structured. Ruby's therapist at treatment told me that she had been sleeping with a thirty-five-year-old man at treatment, and this was strictly prohibited. Ruby assured me that the affair was over and she was ready to be celibate for now and focus on herself and her recovery.

When I spoke to parents like hers, my heart went out to them. Ruby had been involved with another girl for several years, and the girlfriend had abused her very badly, both emotionally and physically. After that relationship ended, Ruby ran off with an older man, and her parents often did not know where she was for weeks, or even months at a time.

I picked Ruby up at treatment. She was lovely looking, but with a very tough edge to her. She had long, flowing blond hair of the type that only one so young can enjoy. The sun hit her highlights, illuminating reddish and light brown tones. She was tiny, but her clear green eyes spoke of the pain she had been through.

"I really don't get along with other girls," she stated when I told her how great her housemates were.

"You'll love my girls," I assured her. "We don't tolerate 'mean girls' behavior at my house. Everyone is excited that you're coming…they're going to welcome you with love and kindness."

She had a piercing through her cheek, an ugly big silver ball telling anyone who looked that she was not some gentle little girl to be messed with. Her clothing was also a mixture of innocence and rebellion—a sweet little flowered sundress that had been washed again and again, the flowers almost rubbed out completely, while her feet were covered by black scuffed-up Doc Martens, which reached several inches above her ankles.

"What's going on with the man who you've been dating?" I asked bluntly, hoping to surprise her with my directness. "Are you still broken up?"

"That's over for good," she assured me. "I told him this morning. He's so old. I don't even know what I was thinking."

Her therapist warned me that they had kicked him out after catching him with Ruby, and I feared he would resurface. "So where is he now?"

"He went back to Chicago."

I hugged her after completing her intake, making certain that she understood the house rules—focusing particularly on no sex, no men, no visitors, and curfews. As a new resident, she would be required to leave the house only with staff or other residents, and I would need to know anytime she left the premises and who she was with as well as when she was home safely.

She rushed out to the smoking area as soon as we finished our meeting, anxious and needing the relief that so many of my women found in smoking. I placed her in a room with another young girl who had been with us for several months. I hoped that they would become fast friends and confidantes, and knew that her roommate would be looking out for Ruby and making sure she complied with all our rules.

The next afternoon I received a call from my house manager.

"Jen just told me that someone was having sex at the pool last night."

"What?" I almost yelled. This was a new one, and I was not pleased.

"Who was it?"

"She said she didn't see who it was."

"Are you kidding me? What don't these women understand about 'no negative contracts'?"

We explained them during our intakes. No negative contracts stated that if someone knew of or suspected a behavior that was against our house rules, they were required to let us know. If they didn't, then they were as guilty of the behavior as the person who had actually done it.

I drove over to the house and called an impromptu meeting with the residents who were home.

"Who heard something at the pool last night?" I asked.

"I thought I heard something, but I was really dead asleep," Karin, one of the elder residents, said. "I went to the bathroom at about 3:00 a.m., and I definitely heard something strange going on at the pool, but I was too tired to investigate."

"Jen?"

"I went out to have a smoke but heard something at the pool, and it was definitely someone having sex, so I shut the door and came back inside."

I looked at them with disbelief. "How many people were having sex out there?"

"It seemed like a man and a woman," Jen said.

"Why didn't someone call me?" I asked, completely frustrated. *How could I blame somebody if I didn't have any proof?* "Why didn't you take a picture and send it to me?"

Three women in total had heard or seen something, but none of them could verify who it was. I was sure it was Ruby since we had never encountered anything like this before her arrival, but I couldn't verify this. I reminded the women that if anything like this ever happened again, I would need to know immediately.

The next morning, Ruby's roommate called and told me that two men had pulled up in our driveway after curfew the night before and that Ruby had left the house with them. This was another complete breach of her contract.

I drove back to the house and went into Ruby's room.

"We need to talk, Ruby."

"Okay."

"I hear that you were outside by the pool two nights ago having sex on a chaise lounge."

"That's a complete lie! I was asleep in my bed!" Her roommate had reported that Ruby's bed had not been slept in either of the two nights that she had been in residence.

"And who were the two guys who came over last night and picked you up?" I continued.

"Nobody picked me up!" she insisted. "I don't know what you're talking about!"

"Where's the guy from treatment that you said you broke up with?" I asked her.

"I have no idea!" she insisted.

"Well then, why are there over twenty phone calls between you and him since you left treatment two days ago and thirty-two text messages?"

"How would you have my phone records?" She was furious now, realizing that the gig was up.

"Your father gave them to me. He still pays your bill. He can see every single text and call."

Her parents and brother had flown down from Connecticut the day before to see her, so I was able to hand her over to them. The looks on their faces when they picked her up were enough to break my heart. The next time I heard from them they wanted me to send a bunch of her belongings to an address in Montana, where she was living with the man from treatment—the same man she had been having sex with by the pool at my sober house. In her haste to pack up, she had forgotten them. Her Doc Martens were among the items she had left behind.

The women in my houses must have sponsors while they live with us. They work their steps and attend meetings. Still, some of them blame me when they don't stay sober.

"You're making me want to drink right now!" a beautiful young woman named Justine said to me one day, anger spewing from her hazel eyes. Her roommate had found a bottle of wine in Justine's closet and called me immediately. I breathalyzed Justine as soon as I could, and she blew a 0.02. Not drunk, but a hint of alcohol there—enough to know that something was going on.

"I'm asking you if this wine is yours, Justine?" Her pretty face was blotchy, and I could see that she had been picking at her skin.

"No, it's not mine!" she yelled. "I have sixty days sober today!"

"So why are you blowing a 0.02?"

"It must be the kombucha!"

"Justine, kombucha has alcohol in it. You're not allowed to drink that." No kava, no kombucha, no vanilla extract, no mouthwash with alcohol in it. We laid all of this out clearly when we did our intakes with each resident.

"I didn't know that," she said, looking deflated. Her eyes were ringed with red, and she looked exhausted. She was slumping down on her bed, but her body, clad in tight yoga clothing, was still perfect.

"No more kombucha. Now give me a hug." I walked over and hugged her, putting love into her heart. "I'm giving you love. I promised to love you until you can love yourself."

Justine laughed a little and hugged me back.

I called her therapist to let her know about the kombucha. We agreed to keep a close eye on Justine, but we weren't able to keep her sober.

In A.A., we are told that one drink is too many and a hundred is never enough. Our disease wants to kill us, and the mental obsession continues to tell us that we're cured now—we can have just one drink again or one drug. If we are truly addicted, our brains never go back to so-called normal drinking or recreational drug use. I have watched people die, over and over. I hear people saying that we can have alcohol or drugs and nothing else, or we can put down alcohol and drugs and have everything else. Our addictions kept us trapped in our own prisons, unable to live life fully. Today I choose everything else.

It Smells Like Poop in Here

When I was a young girl, I used to tell boys that boy farts smelled like poop and girl farts smelled like flowers. So concerned was I with protecting this illusion that I wouldn't fart or poop anywhere when other people were around. Eating in front of guys was another thing that I believed to be unfeminine, so I would graze like a baby fawn if guys were around—lettuce, bananas, apples—only low-calorie, healthy foods entered my mouth in mixed company.

Cindi, an older girl in our neighborhood, taught me how to diet when I was seven. She was twelve at the time. Cindi was thin and beautiful, and I looked up to her as the sister I never had. She had shared her Barbies with me, and now that I was seven, she shared her weight secrets. I had gotten a little bit chubby while away at sleepaway camp that summer, and when my mom took me shopping for back-to-school clothing, she was appalled.

"We're going to have to buy you elastic waist pants," she said, walking quickly past the desirable pants with zippers and snaps.

"I want these!" I insisted, pulling at a pair of thin jeans.

"They're not going to fit you," my mother insisted. "These Danskin pants will be much more comfortable."

I was mortified. Not only did I have to wear shoes with "cookies" in them, because my feet were somewhat flat, but now I was going to be wearing stretch pants that would show every little lump and bump of fat on my body. All the cool girls would be wearing penny loafers and jeans, and I would be in my orthotic shoes and navy blue dance pants. *Nobody is going to want to play with me.*

Cindi's diet consisted of two things: Tab (the old-fashioned Diet Coke in the pink cans) and grapefruit with Sweet'n Low on top. This diet filled me up, because I drank about six cans of Tab a day. I quickly dropped the unwanted pounds and was allowed to buy jeans again. No penny loafers yet, but I wasn't going to be a misfit any more.

The "Cindi diet" also gave me gas, but I was very careful not to fart in front of anybody. Many of the diets that I have tried throughout my life have caused flatulence, constipation, diarrhea, and terrible stomach pains. When I started dating guys in high school and beyond, I suffered from terrible cramps because I never allowed myself to fart or poop when I was with them. Sometimes I would lie in my bed for hours after a long date, flat on my stomach, hoping for the pain to subside. In the privacy of my room, with my en suite bathroom, I could do whatever I wanted without worrying about being unladylike.

Cohabitation and marriage ruined all this for me. It's impossible not to fart or poop when you live with somebody full-time. This is particularly true when you get pregnant. Pregnancy farts are the worst things I have ever smelled, and with age and maturity I have accepted that bowel movements are a part of normal life. My food neuroses have also dissipated, allowing me to pig out from time to time in front of anyone. In recovery I have learned that what other people think of me is none of my business. Surely if people are judging me for what I eat, that is their problem, since I don't suffer from any eating disorders or weight issues.

My sober houses have plenty of bathrooms, but almost all of them are shared by more than one woman. I knew that

I wanted to offer homes that provided privacy and comfort, but some of the issues that have come up since the beginning were things that I had never planned for.

"It smells really bad in here!" one of my early residents named Nancy announced when I arrived for bed and chore checks one morning.

I sniffed deeply, and I did smell something poop-like.

"You're right," I said. "My nose is really good since I stopped doing coke. It does smell funky in here."

"Sometimes it's fine," Nancy continued, "but then it's back all of a sudden. It's been going on for days."

I walked around the room, sniffing things out. *Who would have known that sniffing for poop was going to be one of my responsibilities when I opened a sober house?* The bedroom smelled okay, and so did the closet. The odor was definitely emanating from the bathroom. I poked around in the trash can and found several bloody sanitary pads. *Why would somebody throw these in the bathroom trash? Why wouldn't they wrap them up and take them out to the garage trash cans?*

A young girl named Pam had moved in with Nancy recently, and apparently she was the culprit. Pam was nineteen and had never lived away from home before. She probably didn't even know that she could have been using tampons by then, or at least cleaning up properly after herself.

I found Pam sitting alone outside, smoking a cigarette and listening to music with headphones on. I tapped her gently on the arm.

"Oh, hi!" she said. She gave me a big smile, showing her perfect white teeth. She was exotic-looking, with darkly tanned skin and beautiful straight thick brown hair that hung to her waist. Only the ugly piercings between her lips and her nose spoke of some of the things she had been through. They made her look tough and unapproachable, but she was neither. Pam was scared and broken inside.

"Hi, Pam! How are you?"

I gave her a hug. She was so young, and had been through a lot. A car accident when she was sixteen had resulted in prescriptions for opiates, and by the time she was forced into treatment by her parents, she was a full-fledged heroin addict. She shot herself up all the time and had started prostituting to pay for her habit. Her parents were lovely, and so was she, and I wanted her to get better.

I knew that I needed to tread carefully with her so that she would trust me.

We caught up for a couple of minutes, and then I got to the point.

"I was in your bathroom a little while ago, and I noticed that there were some sanitary pads in the trash can. Were they yours?"

"I guess so," she said. "I am on my period."

"Since you're sharing a bathroom, would you mind wrapping those in something and putting them in the outdoor trash cans please? I don't want other people to have to see them."

"Okay," she agreed. "I've never shared a bathroom before, except in my last sober house, and that place was a dump. I do have to tell you, though, I think there's something wrong with Nancy."

"What do you mean?" I asked her.

"I think she's leaking something onto her bed. Something was dripping out of her when she went to the bathroom last night, and it's probably on her bedding too. It was bright yellow, like an egg yolk."

"Did she wipe up the floor?"

"Kind of, but you'd better check her bed."

I went in and looked at Nancy's bed. The comforter looked okay. I was afraid to look underneath though. *What if she had dripped something, and it had leaked through the sheets to the mattress cover and even the mattress?* I worried. Not sure what to do, I reviewed Nancy's file and saw that she had severe liver damage and some other medical issues. I was afraid that I might catch something from her and that her roommate could get sick too.

I called my sober house mentor, and he answered right away.

"Have you ever had someone dripping stuff into their bedding?" I asked him. *I wasn't even sure if guys leaked the same way that women did.*

"What are you talking about, girlfriend?" he asked me, laughing.

"It's not funny," I replied, laughing despite myself. "I think one of my women may be leaking bright-yellow fluid onto her bed, and I'm afraid to look under the covers."

"Sounds like a HAZMAT situation to me."

"What do you mean?" I asked, picturing men in head-to-toe protective gear, with masks covering their faces. "Have you ever had this?"

"Nope. Told you I don't work with women for a reason."

I waited until nobody was in or near Nancy and Pam's room, and I went in and closed their door behind me. This sneaking had me feeling like a thief, wondering what the women would think if they saw what I was doing. I lifted the comforter up from the top and pulled down the top sheet. There was a brown towel covering the sheets—the towel and sheets were wet. We didn't have any brown towels in my house. Our color scheme was beachy—blues, greens, and whites. *Funny that she bought a brown towel. Poop color.* I smelled the sheets, but they didn't have any specific odor. I pulled the sheets up and looked at the mattress pad, which appeared to be dry and unstained. *Well, I don't smell any poop,* I realized with relief.

After covering the evidence of my tampering, I went out to find Nancy. She was sitting on the meditation beach, reading a paperback.

"Hey, I spoke to Pam about the pads. She's going to make sure to dispose of them properly from now on. I didn't tell her that you told me. I just told her that I noticed them in the trash can in your bathroom."

"Thanks," Nancy said, looking relieved.

"Your bed looked a little bumpy," I told her. "I pulled up your covers and saw a brown towel on your sheets, and it was kind of wet. Are you having some leakage or something?" I asked her in my most loving voice.

"No!" she said immediately. "I sleep with a water bottle in my bed, and it must have leaked."

"Okay," I told her. "I can buy you a plastic mattress liner to go under your mattress cover if you want one," I offered.

"I don't need it," she assured me.

"No issues with your liver problem?"

"No, not at all."

Crisis diverted, I thought as I drove away from the house. I was going to take a nice hot shower as soon as I got home. Somehow I had managed decades of summer camps, college dorms, and shared apartments without encountering these issues, but owning a sober house was bringing forth a whole new set of issues.

Over-the-counter laxatives are also a constant problem. My women always seem to be complaining of constipation or weight gain, and buying laxatives is one of their favorite pastimes. I don't allow the women to have them, unless they are prescribed by a doctor. I could probably open a small laxative store with all the laxatives that we have confiscated from residents. Learning how to move their bowels through healthier eating is something we talk about with women privately whenever we find them hidden away, which is pretty often.

I have bought high-tech blenders for the houses and taught my residents how to make healthy green juices, which are good for digestion. A sober nutritionist has visited and helped the residents to understand healthy eating. We try to show them how to shop and cook simply and nutritionally when they are open to it. More often than not, though, pizza or Chinese food is being delivered, and the microwave is running, heating up salty, fattening meals. Until I can afford to hire a full-time chef, this is bound to be something that we will continue to grapple with.

Our odor issues never seem to stop. When Megan moved in, she was skinny as a rail and highly nervous. She reminded me of Olive Oyl from *Popeye*—tall, thin, and pale, with straight black hair cut into a blunt bob. She looked borderline anorexic, but her medical records were clear, and she did not report any eating issues during her intake. She was recovering from addiction to alcohol and drugs.

The complaints started right away.

"Megan is throwing up," one of her housemates reported during Megan's first week at the house.

"How do you know?" I asked.

"She eats all day and night and then goes into the bathroom, and I hear her gagging."

I sat down with Megan and asked her how things were going, and she reported that she was doing well.

"Your housemates say you're throwing up after you eat. Is this true?"

"No, it's not true!" she answered. Her face was red, and she was angry. "I don't have an eating disorder. I'm just thin."

"Why are you gagging in the bathroom all the time?"

"I have a bad stomach," she said. "I get nauseous after I eat, but I'm not throwing up! I'm going to move out!" she cried. "I don't need this!"

I assured her that I believed her and that she was safe with us. Her housemates were told to stop gossiping about Megan and to focus on themselves.

The reports continued, culminating in her housemates calling a meeting with me a few weeks later to do a semi-intervention.

"Ladies," I told them. "I have spoken to Megan. I've spoken to her mother and her sisters. I've spoken to her therapist. She does not have an eating disorder. She's here to stay sober from alcohol and drugs. Please stop gossiping about her and make her feel safe."

Before long, Megan's roommate told me that Megan was having explosive diarrhea, and it was getting all over the bathroom. It was on the bathroom walls, toilet, and floor. It was also on the bedroom floor, where it had dripped out of her when she was going to the bathroom in the middle of the night. Once again, I went over and inspected her bed. There were towels under her sheets— big bath sheets. There was no poop smell, and I didn't find any stains. It was hard to believe that I was actually smelling another mattress, but her roommate kept complaining that the room and bathroom were unsanitary and smelly.

My house manager and I met with Megan.

"Are you having diarrhea?" I asked.

"Yes. I have irritable bowel syndrome. I've had it for my whole life."

"We're going to buy you some Clorox wipes, a toilet brush, and bathroom cleaner," I told her. "Please be sure to clean up after yourself."

"My stomach issues have ruined my life!" Megan said. "I can't even have a relationship with a man because of this. Part of the reason I became an addict was because of this." She was as close to breaking down as I had seen her. "I can move out," she said, "I found a house that has private bathrooms."

"We don't want you to leave," I told her. "We love you." Megan was one of the neater and less needy residents we had housed, and I didn't want her to feel unwanted. "Just be sure to see your GI doctor soon, honey," I told her. "Maybe there are certain foods you should avoid, or something you can take to help you feel better."

We kept Megan's bathroom loaded with cleaning supplies, and the complaints lessened. Nobody got very close to Megan during her stay with us, but I felt sorry for her and wanted her to be safe and sober. She had lost her family to her addiction, and I wanted to see her reconciled with them and living a more meaningful life. *Why did I have sober houses if I couldn't support women who needed help, regardless of their health issues?* Eventually, a single room with a private bathroom opened up, and I moved her in there. New residents still reported occasional gagging sounds, but Megan looked healthy and was never ill. She lived with us for a year. She went to meetings every day, worked her steps with a sponsor, and was able to move back home with her family. She has been sober ever since. She still has stomach issues, but she has her own bathroom, and nobody is bothering her about them.

A.A. is a program of progress, not perfection. Some of us are sicker than others. I'm just trying to provide women with a safe and nurturing place where they can learn how to live their lives clean and sober. Many of my residents need more than a 12-step program—they go to psychiatrists, medical doctors, therapists, acupuncturists, personal trainers, and nutritionists. One thing is certain though, and that is none of their problems are going to get better by picking up a drink or a drug. We stay sober by working a program, one day at a time. And things never get worse. My worst day sober is better than my best day high, and most of my residents would agree.

The Women Who Beach and Botox

Staying sober is not easy. In the rooms of Alcoholics Anonymous, we learn some of the things that have worked for other people in recovery. *Meeting makers make it*, we are told. In my first week of recovery, I heard that going to ninety meetings in ninety days was the number one predictor for staying sober. I have no idea if this is true, but I decided to try it. Surely too many meetings couldn't hurt me. During my *90 in 90*, I fell in love with meetings so I have never stopped going.

"I spent a lot more than an hour a day drinking and getting high," a guy from my daily A.A. meeting would say. "Spending an hour a day at a meeting has kept me sober for almost five years."

Stick with the winners, I heard. So I followed the simple instructions that were given out so freely in my meetings, and I did what other people did as long as they were sober and seemed happy.

We were also told to work the 12-steps of recovery with a sponsor and to help others. All these things have helped me to live a happy, joyous, and free life in recovery so I insist that women in my houses do the same. (Yes, I have two houses now—The Frog Pad 2 opened in early 2016 a year after I opened my first house.)

"This is a simple program for complex people," my first sponsor told me, and I hear this in the rooms often. I have found it relatively easy to stay sober by following the simple things that were recommended:

Go to meetings.

Get a sponsor.

Work the 12-steps.

Help others.

"Ninety meetings in ninety days," I told my first resident Kerri. "This is not a requirement of my house, but I was told that people who do a ninety in ninety stay sober longer than those who do anything else." I required that residents attended a minimum of five meetings weekly, but I did believe that ninety in ninety was a great tool.

"Even rehab?" she asked me.

Kerri had gone to a luxury rehab in South Florida earlier in the year. They allowed cell phones and computers. The patients could go out to dinner every night, and working out with personal trainers daily was included in their exorbitant treatment fees. Kerri particularly liked eating out in Palm Beach. Café Boulud was her favorite restaurant, and she dined there about three times a week. Even by Palm Beach standards, this was a very expensive restaurant.

"Yes," I answered. "Even rehab. There's no question that rehab teaches people about the disease of alcoholism, but it's what we do afterward that truly matters." Rehab hadn't kept Kerri sober, so maybe ninety meetings in ninety days would.

"Want to have dinner with me tonight?" Kerri asked me on the phone about a week after she had moved in.

"I can't," I told her. The truth was that I only ate at Café Boulud about once a year, on a special occasion. Anthony's Coal Oven Pizza or dinner at home were more my speed on a typical night.

"Okay, well, I'm taking Uber there then," she informed me. "I'll call you when I get home."

"What did you do after the meeting this morning?" I asked.

"Oh, I found an amazing place for a colonic. I'm going again tomorrow."

Kerri was incredibly tiny, and she barely ate. She exercised like a fiend, and definitely had food and exercise issues as well as alcoholism.

"Why?" I asked.

"Oh, they're great," she told me knowingly. "I've been so backed up since you took my laxatives away."

"Laxatives aren't allowed in the house for a reason, Kerri," I reminded her. "You need to eat normally and let your body stabilize."

Many women abuse laxatives, and this is even more prevalent for women in recovery than the average population. They feel that taking laxatives will make them lose weight, and when they stop working, they take greater quantities to achieve the desired effect.

"I also went to the beach again," she continued, ignoring my mini lecture. "There were some really cute guys there, drinking beer at like eleven in the morning."

"I hope you didn't speak to them."

"I didn't. I had my headphones in my ears, and I was listening to music."

Kerri loved going to yoga with me. One of the things that I offered as part of a resident's rent was regular yoga classes with an amazing teacher named Seth, and Kerri liked him so much that she immediately started to take private lessons with him. This was another thing that I would treat myself to once or twice a year, but she was doing privates with him every other day. At one hundred and fifty dollars a session, this was adding up, but money never seemed to be an issue for her. Her rich older husband paid the bills.

Seth's classes had been extremely therapeutic for me in my early recovery.

"If you see somebody doing something that you wish you could do, just close your eyes and imagine yourself doing it. You'll get all the benefits that they get doing the actual pose," he told his classes.

"This is really just a breathing class," he repeated every week. "If all you do is sit on your mat and breathe through your nose, you're doing yoga."

Seth had a gift. I could bring women to his classes, and he would be drawn to the ones who were broken, even if they were practicing across the room from me. Several times he approached these women after class and spoke to them. "I know," he told them, looking directly into their eyes with his clear blue ones. "You're going to be fine." Seth could sense their suffering, and let them know that he felt it too and they would be okay.

"If you're thinking about something other than yoga right now...," he would say invariably when I was thinking about what I needed to buy at the supermarket after class or what I needed to discuss with someone that afternoon. "Just give yourself a break from yourself. Tell yourself—not now—I'm doing yoga."

This always put a big smile on my face and put me right back where I needed to be, which was in the moment, practicing yoga. This mindfulness, or living in the present moment, was a practice that was very important to me in my recovery, so I brought Seth into the lives of my residents, and many of them had found it extremely healing as well.

A week or so later, I was meeting one-on-one with Kerri.

"How is IOP going?" I asked.

"Oh, I stopped going."

"What?" I was shocked. Due to her relapse in New York, I had made IOP a criterion of her moving into my house. "When?"

"I stopped going a few days ago. It was a waste of time. Yoga and going to the beach make me feel so much better."

"Kerri, you can't just stop going to IOP without discussing it with me. You're not going to stay sober by working on your tan and doing yoga." She had also starting making herself throw up after eating at Café Boulud, and admitted this to me a few nights earlier. I made it clear to her that purging was not allowed in my house.

"I don't agree. I need to do what makes me happy. IOP was depressing me."

Kerri went home a few days later because she refused to comply with my house rules. She didn't want to get a sponsor, and she refused to go to IOP. She had paid for a full month, but she didn't care. Her husband was paying anyway, and she said she missed her daughters.

"I'm going to take yoga teacher training when I get home," she told me as I drove her back to the airport in West Palm Beach.

Kerri called me about nine months after she left The Frog Pad. Yoga hadn't kept her sober. She had recently completed a ninety-day treatment program in Pennsylvania and said that she was finally ready to work a program.

"Thank you so much for everything you taught me," she said before hanging up. "You were right that I needed to work a program in order to stay sober." She was ready to begin going to meetings and find a sponsor and work the steps.

Then there was Michelle. She couldn't afford the full rent at my house and begged me to give her a partial scholarship. She had lost her high-paying job due to her addiction, and her boyfriend had broken up with her after one too many broken promises about staying clean. Her addictions were to alcohol, Xanax, and cocaine, and she was struggling to recover. I decided to help her out, believing her when she said that she was willing to go to any lengths to stay sober. I hoped that she would learn what she needed in my sober house, so that she could get back to whatever it was that she wanted for the rest of her life.

Michelle was in her early thirties—a very attractive woman with long blond hair and a sexy, curvy body. She loved to show off her ample cleavage, wearing bright, tight tank tops that barely contained her. She had a pierced belly button, and a tongue ring, which she played with inces-

santly, suggesting what kind of pleasure it could give someone else. Her shorts rarely covered her butt, allowing others
to enjoy viewing the labors of her many hours in the gym
every week.

One day she came home, and her lips were black and
blue.

"What happened to you?" I asked.

"Nothing." She opened the refrigerator and removed a
Red Bull, opening it loudly and taking a big swallow.

"Your lips are all black and blue. Did you fall down or
something?"

"She got lip injections today," Gayle, one of my wealth-
ier residents, said. "That's why she's all swollen."

*Great, another one who couldn't pay full rent but could
somehow afford to pay for lip injections.*

"Well, *you* got Botox," Michelle countered to Gayle.

Gayle could well afford Botox, not that I thought it was a
good use of her time to be getting injections while her children
were up in Connecticut without their mother. She received a
hefty alimony payment every month, which seemed to burn
a hole in her pocket as soon as it arrived. Shopping at Boca
Town Center was one of her favorite pastimes, and she was

known to come home with bags of clothing, which she would then try on for all the residents, getting their opinions on what looked best on her. Gayle already had a few too many procedures done, leaving her naturally pretty face looking a bit like a bumpy caricature of a once-beautiful woman. She was in her late forties, but all the work she had done left her looking more like a sixty-five-year-old who had lived a difficult life.

"I'm a lot older than you, Michelle," Gayle said in a whiny voice. "How am I going to find another man if I don't keep myself looking young?"

Gayle also had tremendous breasts, but hers were implants, and she, too, loved going to mixed NA and A.A. meetings wearing very little to cover them up. She was chunky, but the guys didn't seem to mind. She would stand outside the meetings before they started and after they ended, smoking her vapor cigarette and batting her eyelash extensions. A lot of my women had started smoking vapes as a way to cut down on cigarettes. They were very popular in Delray, especially among people in recovery. There were stores that sold nothing but vapes and juice, and a lot of recovering addicts worked in these stores and hung out in them. Rather than hanging out in bars, they sat around in the vape stores on weekend nights, blowing giant clouds of fragrant smoke and listening to music.

"No new relationships in the first year," I reminded her. It was generally believed that getting into a relationship in early recovery could lead to relapse. The new partner often takes the focus off the recovery program. Couples often relapse together, and breakups can also lead to negative self-talk and relapses.

"Oh, I'm just practicing," she said. "None of these guys can afford me."

"Have you ladies found sponsors yet?"

"I have a number of someone," Michelle said.

"Call her today and then tell me what she says. And you, Gayle?"

"No."

"You have until Friday. No more trips to the dermatologist for you two until you have sponsors and are working your steps."

Tanning salons and self-tanners were also big among my residents. One of them, Karin, even got a job at a nearby tanning salon just so she could tan for free every day. She was twenty years old and a pretty young girl with big green eyes that really popped as she got tanner and tanner.

"Why don't you just go outside?" I asked her one day. "We live in South Florida. It's sunny all the time."

"I just love tanning booths," she replied. "They're so relaxing."

Apparently she also loved the fact that the guy she worked with was a willing sex partner. She didn't come home from work one night and didn't reply to my texts or phone calls. It was a Saturday night, and curfew was midnight. She still wasn't home the next morning.

"Karin's missing," I told her dad on the phone the next morning when she still wasn't answering my calls.

"I'm so sorry," he replied. He wasn't even concerned— although she was only twenty years old she had been in and out of treatment centers for several years, and *running* was her specialty.

"Karin's missing," I informed her roommates the next morning when I came over to dispense medications and do bed and chore checks. We kept all prescriptions locked up in safes, and residents had to be out of bed by 9:00 a.m. with their beds made and chores completed by 9:30 a.m. "Does anyone know where she is?"

"What? She just moved in," one of the other residents said.

"Yes, well, she never came home last night, and she isn't answering her calls or text messages."

"She texted me last night," her roommate finally admitted. "And she was bragging yesterday before work that she was going out to 'get some good cock' after work."

"Well, she's missing now." The way some of these women spoke about sex was a little too crass for me, and I'm no prude. "I really don't care if she wanted to have sex, but she didn't ask for permission for an overnight, and she could have had sex before midnight and still been home before curfew."

At our mandatory house meeting that Friday morning, we discussed Karin's departure from the house.

"If you can't follow the simple rules at this house, you are going to have a very difficult time staying sober when you leave," I told the room filled with my residents. Sixteen pairs of eyes looked back at me. "This isn't a lockdown rehab," I reminded them. "This is a bridge back to life. All of you deserve to have beautiful lives without drugs and alcohol. As long as you immerse yourselves in this simple program, anything is possible."

A hand shot up. It was Gayle.

"Yes, Gayle?"

"Your website and brochure say that going to the beach and doing yoga help keep you sober."

I saw a number of heads nodding in agreement.

"Are you kidding me? Those are things that are therapeutic and a wonderful addition to a recovery program. Going to a tanning salon or to the beach isn't going to keep you sober unless you do *what*?" I looked around the room, hoping for some recovery-focused answers.

"Talk to someone," one of them called out.

"Talk to someone in recovery," I said. "Good one. What else?"

"Go to meetings," someone else piped in.

"Exactly. What else?"

"Yoga?" somebody asked.

"Yoga's great, but not unless you also have a sponsor, work your steps, do service work, and help another person in recovery." Sometimes I felt like a broken record, but it amazed me that these women actually sat around critiquing my brochures and website rather than going to meetings or finding themselves a good sponsor.

"Who here has a service commitment?" I asked the group.

"What's that?" a newer resident asked.

"Making coffee at a meeting, being a greeter, chairing a meeting," I suggested. Nobody raised her hand this time.

"We can't keep what we don't give away," I told them. "My first sponsor told me that the way I could pay him back for helping to save my life would be to help another addict who was sick and suffering as soon as I was able to." I took this very seriously, getting my first service commitment when I had less than three months sober.

"I was the secretary for a Friday night C.A. meeting for six months," I told my women. "Every week I passed the basket and asked people to give what they could to help support the meeting. I wasn't even allowed to count the money, but I took this commitment very seriously, and it kept me sober for six months. Every time I thought of drinking or drugging, I pictured the people at that six p.m. meeting, wondering where I was when it was time to pass the basket. What would they think if I wasn't there? This literally helped to keep me sober."

A few heads nodded, seeming to understand this concept.

"My husband picked me up after that meeting," I reflected. "It didn't end until seven fifteen, and he wasn't thrilled by my commitment. I needed it though—Friday evenings had been one of my favorite times to get high."

More nodding heads surrounded me in the living room of House One.

"We're going to have Tacos and Tattoos on Tuesday," my house manager reminded them. "Who's in?"

Most of the hands shot up. I had started Tacos and Tattoos when I first opened, bringing over the ingredients for healthy tacos, with the residents who could join in the potluck. I brought metallic temporary tattoos, and we played music, danced and ate tacos, and decorated each other with shiny tattoos that lasted weeks rather than a lifetime.

"Some people call this the Fun House," I told them. "This is said as a criticism. My feeling is that if we are miserable in our recovery, we aren't going to want to stay sober."

As long as my women were complying with the rules of the house, I wanted to expose them to fun in their recovery. That's what it was all about. Fellowship and fun with other women in recovery was something I was promoting—women who would tell us *what we needed to hear*, not just *what we wanted to hear*.

"Going to the beach and getting Botox does not get us sober," I reminded them as we began to move the furniture against the walls for in-house yoga.

"But it makes us happy!" Michelle yelled out, laughing.

No Mean Girls Allowed

Women are not always nice to one another, and living together in a house filled with other women is not something that many are happy about. No addict or alcoholic asked to have this disease, and when we get sober, we are essentially giving up our best friends—alcohol and drugs. These substances had filled a void for us. They had been our solution to every problem. We drank or used to deal with life. When they are removed from our lives, we are left to learn how to deal with life sober. This is very difficult for most, especially in early recovery.

When women interview and tour my sober houses, I tell them that no *mean girls* are allowed. Everyone is broken when they arrive at my houses. I believe that being treated with love, compassion, and kindness is essential in the healing process.

"We are all birds with at least one broken wing," I tell potential residents and their families when I speak to them before admission. "My goal is to help women heal, and if they can't be kind and accepting of each other, they will be asked to leave. As many women have been asked to leave my houses for this as those who have relapsed."

The younger women can be vicious at times. They want to hang out and room together, but this often results in terrible fighting. One resident Melissa was going through a breakup with her boyfriend—she was heartbroken, of course—and her nineteen-year-old roommate Stella did nothing but talk about how in love she and her boyfriend were. Their third roommate Carolina was siding with Stella.

"Why does Stella think telling me this stuff about how in love she is will help me?" Melissa asked me. "I come home from work and try to tell her how upset I am, and all she does is show me pictures of her disgusting boyfriend. He looks like he's on steroids!"

Melissa was gorgeous. She had long blond hair, filled with natural highlights, and her blue eyes were big and round, shining out of her perfect face like gemstones. Her twenty-two-year-old body was flawless, and she did absolutely nothing to look this way.

Stella was madly in love with her rehab guy and could think of little else. She didn't want to listen to Melissa's woes and began gossiping about her with Carolina.

"I saw some texts between Carolina and Stella," Melissa told me. "Carolina showed them to me. They're conspiring against me. They say one thing to my face and then stab me in the back whenever I'm not around. I can't take this anymore! And I heard them talking about me after I left the room last night. They were nice to my face, but as soon as I walked out, they started laughing and talking shit about me."

Melissa showed me the text messages, and they were harsh. She had taken a screen shot of them and sent them to her phone. I got the three of them together to talk.

"Ladies," I said, "you all need to treat each other with love and kindness here. That's what sober living is about. All of you need support from one another."

"All Melissa does is complain about her stupid breakup," Stella told me afterward. "She's such a Debbie Downer."

"Try to imagine yourself in her shoes," I told her. "You're falling in love and she's heartbroken right now. Pray for her."

The backstabbing continued almost immediately after I left the house. Melissa called me, sobbing.

"I can't live with these girls! I hate other girls. They've always been mean to me my whole life."

"Maybe they're jealous of you. You're so incredibly beautiful. Just try to focus on your recovery right now."

"Girls have always hated me. That's why I just hang out with guys."

When Stella wouldn't stop gossiping and sending nasty texts about Melissa to Carolina, I asked her to find another place to live. She moved in with her boyfriend, and they both started drinking immediately. I moved Melissa into another room with a much-older resident. They got along beautifully. There was no competition between them, and they treated each other kindly. They remain friendly today, despite their forty-five-year age difference. They are both sober and enjoying life in the real world.

Older women can be awful too. I had a resident from New York named Nancy. She was the mom of three and had left her family to come down to Florida for rehab. Her husband was not ready for her to come home and insisted that she find a sober house to live in. Nancy was sarcastic and funny, but her words were often hurtful, and she would drive other women to tears.

"I'm moving out," another resident named Wendy told me one morning. "I cannot live in a house with Nancy any longer. She's making me want to drink, and I can't risk my sobriety."

"Why didn't you tell me about this?" I asked.

I didn't want to lose Wendy. She had moved in less than a month earlier and was planning to stay with us for at least six months. She was responsible and compliant, while Nancy was short-tempered and difficult to deal with.

"I'm an adult," she told me. "I don't want to be tattling on other people. I found an apartment, and I signed a lease."

"If you had discussed this with me, I would have addressed it with Nancy directly," I explained. "If anyone should move out, it's her."

"Well, I'm leaving. I'm giving you my two weeks' notice, but I'm moving in with my sponsor today until my apartment is ready."

I met with Nancy and told her that her behaviors had made Wendy so uncomfortable that she was moving out.

"She's not moving out because of me," Nancy said. "She hates you."

"What are you talking about? That's a terrible thing to say."

"Yeah, well, you don't live here, Mallory. A lot of people hate you!"

I called a house meeting.

"Ladies," I said, "I understand that some of you are saying that you hate me. This is my house, and if you have a problem with me, you should go somewhere else. All I'm trying to do here is help you and provide you with beautiful and sober lives. There are plenty of other places you can go if you're unhappy."

"We love each other," Nancy said. "We just don't like you."

"That's enough, Nancy," I cut in. "We can discuss this privately."

After the meeting, Nancy told me that she had just been kidding. She gave me a hug and told me she loved me.

"Nancy, you can't say things like that here. I own these houses, and your behavior in the meeting was completely unacceptable. One more cruel comment and you're going to have to move out."

Another resident named Lisa asked to speak to me.

"I'm moving out too if Nancy doesn't," she said. "She's crazy. She lashes out at us, and then when we get upset, she tries to hug us and tell us she was just joking. And none of us hate you. She's the only one who says that."

Nancy had a bipolar diagnosis in addition to her drug and alcohol addictions. I told her to meet with her psychiatrist to see if her medications needed to be adjusted. A few days later, I came over and the furniture in the house had all been rearranged. It looked terrible.

"Who rearranged this furniture?" I asked the women who were there.

"Nancy did." Nancy was sitting on the couch watching television, looking smug.

"Nancy, please put the furniture back to the way it was. This is not your house."

Nancy put the furniture back, muttering under her breath while I watched.

The next day I went over to give a tour. When I walked inside with my prospective resident, the furniture had been rearranged again. Nancy was sitting on the couch, once again watching TV.

"Nancy," I said. "Did you move the furniture again?" I also noticed that she had moved artwork around this time.

"Yes, I did," she said, with a little smile on her face.

"Put it back the way it was, right now," I told her and resumed giving my tour.

When the prospective resident left, Nancy confronted me.

"How dare you humiliate me like that in front of a stranger? Is that what you call love and kindness, Mallory?"

"Nancy, I told you not to rearrange the furniture again. This is my house. You don't just walk into somebody's house and move their paintings and furniture around."

"You don't even live here! It was much cozier the way I made it."

I asked Nancy to find another place to live the third time she rearranged the furniture. The house went back to normal as soon as she left. I will not tolerate disrespect from my women, toward me, or most importantly, toward one another.

The first *mean girl* who moved in was named Dina. I thought she was trouble the first time I met her. She and her mom came over for a tour a few days before Dina was being discharged from rehab. It was clear that she was spoiled and her mother could not control her. Dina whined and complained while her mother told me that she could not live with Dina anymore and neither could Dina's dad. Both of Dina's parents lived nearby. They were divorced and fighting over the fact that their youngest daughter kept relapsing and going back to treatment. This time they were insisting that she move into a sober house.

Dina wanted to move into my house because it was brand-new and more luxurious than the other places they had toured. I had been open for almost six months, and despite my initial concerns about her self-entitlement, I agreed to let her move in. She had grown up privileged and was on probation with the law, so she would have serious legal consequences if she drank or used. I explained our house rules to her during her intake and told her that she couldn't leave the house without letting me know where she was going.

I walked into the house on Dina's second day in residence, and she walked right past me and out the front door.

"Dina!" I called after her. "You can't just walk past me like that. Where are you going?"

"My Uber's here."

"I told you that you can't leave the house without telling me," I said to her back. "And don't walk past me without saying hello."

"Fuck you! You're not my mother!"

I called her real mother right away. "She cannot speak to me like this."

"I'm so sorry, Mallory. I'll speak to her."

Dina was very sweet with most of the other residents and became their unofficial house mascot. She was twenty-one years old, and she played up her youth with the older women. Her maturity level was closer to that of a twelve-year-old. With girls closer to her age, she was petty and mean.

"Dina," I told her during one of our constant one-on-ones, "you're making Ally feel left out and horrible. This kind of behavior is not okay here."

"She fucked my boyfriend!" Dina said. "I told her I was in love with him, and she wouldn't stop texting him! I'm not going to be nice to her."

I met with Ally.

"He was my boyfriend first! He didn't even want to fuck her, but she threw herself at him! He thinks she's disgusting."

285

Dina would hook up with random guys she met in meetings, and having sex with them was her version of having a boyfriend. Most of them never came back for seconds, and then she would lie in her bed, heartbroken. She took selfies in her bikinis and underwear and sent them to the guys to try and entice them back for more. When this failed, she cried to her housemates. She also continued to gossip about Ally.

"Ally will never be my friend again!" Dina told me. "Friends don't fuck each other's boyfriends! It's an unwritten rule."

"Stop gossiping about Ally. She has her own version of the story, and being unkind to her is not okay. She feels completely left out."

Dina said nothing, sitting on her bed admiring her manicure.

"You need to stay away from guys right now," I said. "Just focus on your recovery and your IOP."

Shopping was one of her favorite pastimes. Dina got rides to the mall with other residents and then found luxury items that she wanted. Having no money of her own, she would call her mother from the stores, begging for the things she wanted.

"Mommy, there's a Louis Vuitton bag that I *have* to have. Can I put it on your credit card?" (Pause.) "But I *need* it!" she screamed. "I don't have a bag like this!"

Her housemates were embarrassed by this display, moving away from Dina on the floor of Saks Fifth Avenue.

"Get me this bag!" (Another pause.)

Shoppers and staff were staring, but Dina finally plopped her mother's credit card down on the counter. "I'll take it!" she told the saleswoman.

This happened often. Dina would throw public temper tantrums until she got what she wanted.

"She's not going to learn if you keep caving in to her," I told her mother. "You're reinforcing some very negative behaviors."

"I know, but I was at work, and I couldn't deal with her anymore."

"It's easier to say yes than to teach our children properly. You're not doing her a favor here."

"She has always been so difficult. Her older sister has never been like this."

"She isn't going to change if she keeps getting whatever she wants."

Dina lived at The Frog Pad for five months. *It felt like five years.* She remained sober during that time, but she continued to treat me badly, often in front of other residents. Every time I called her mother she begged me to reconsider, and she drove over.

"Just tell me what we need to do," her mother said, sitting once again in our living room with Dina beside her.

"I want to move to Daddy's," Dina said.

"You're not moving anywhere! Your father doesn't want you to live with him."

I finally reached my boiling point. After at least five meetings and a dozen more phone calls with her mother, regarding Dina's *mean-girl* behaviors, she called me a *stupid bitch* during our weekly house meeting. I called her mom and told her that Dina had to go. By cursing me out constantly, she was setting a terrible example.

How dare you kick Dina out of your house? her father texted me a few hours later. This was the first time I had ever heard from him. *You're going to be very sorry about this. I'm going to report you to the authorities.*

I read the text in disbelief. I had put up with his nasty, spoiled daughter for five months and had done nothing unethical.

Her mother texted me next:

I want my security deposit back. Send it immediately.

Residents do not get their security back if they are asked to leave. Dina signed a contract stating this, and you were also aware of this during her interview and intake.

Send me the contract! You will regret this!

I sent her the page of the contract that explained Dina's security deposit.

You're a criminal, her mother wrote back. *I'm going to write to the newspapers about you and blow up social media.*

Dina moved in with her father. I haven't heard from either of her parents again. Dina left me with over two hundred dollars in movie rentals. I took it out of her security deposit.

Animal House or Sober House?

I love animals, especially dogs. At the end of my active addiction, my poor dog Grandpa was anxious and exhausted. Grandpa is a dapple dachshund, and we semi-rescued him from an upscale puppy store in Greenwich Village. My daughter Morgan and I were on a mission to find a little dachshund. One day, while Morgan was at school, I wandered around downtown Manhattan visiting puppy stores.

"Do you have any dachshunds coming in?" I asked the salesperson at our favorite puppy store.

I looked in the cages, and there were a lot of cute (and extremely expensive) puppies for sale, but no dachshunds.

"There's one down in the basement," the guy told me. "I'll go get him."

Down in the basement? Why would a puppy be down there?

"Here he is. Nobody wants him, so I may bring him home myself." The guy looked like he was barely eking out a living, wearing very old-looking jeans, and a faded out T-shirt. His hair was dirty looking, and he seemed to be in his late twenties or early thirties. I worried that he couldn't feed himself, let alone a dog.

"Oh, my god! He's adorable!"

The guy put the puppy down on the floor, and I sat down to play with him.

"I love him!" The puppy was running around and wagging his little tail. He had intelligent-looking dark-brown eyes and had spots in black, tan, and gray.

"Why doesn't anyone want him?"

"He's already over five months old," the guy said. "Most of our puppies sell when they're three or four months. If you want him, I'll give him to you for half price."

"I'm going to pick my daughter up at school and bring her back. If she wants him, you have a deal."

"Oh, Mommy!" Morgan exclaimed a couple of hours later when she met the puppy. "I love him! Can we have him? Please?"

"We can get him, and you can name him." And that's how our dachshund was named Grandpa—I gave free rein to my very original fourteen-year-old.

Grandpa was a great dog, and he loved sleeping with me every night. When Mark moved in, Grandpa burrowed under the covers between us. Like most dogs, he was an excellent sleeper and loved to cuddle.

My drug use threw Grandpa off balance—with me in the bathroom for hours, smoking cigarettes and snorting coke, and Mark in the bedroom fast asleep, Grandpa didn't know which way to go. He would scratch on the bathroom door, wanting to check on me, and I would let him in—trying to be quiet so as not to wake Mark. Grandpa watched me from the bathroom rug, looking worried, and then scratched at the inside the door, wanting to go back to bed. He seemed to be begging me to come to bed with him each time he sadly left the bathroom and headed back to our bed. He seemed as anxious and depressed as I was. My addiction was upsetting the balance of his otherwise tranquil life.

When I got sober, Grandpa was with me every day. He was always home, waiting for me when I finished with my IOP and meetings. My cravings were often obsessive in the early months, and Grandpa would sit on my bed with me every evening while I texted and called people from the program. His soft fur comforted me, and I petted him so often that sometimes I thought his fur would rub away completely.

"You're my best friend," I told him often, with tears in my eyes. "I'm so sorry that I tortured you."

It's okay, he seemed to tell me with his beautiful eyes. *We're okay now.*

I often say that I couldn't have made it through my first ninety days of sobriety without Grandpa. The simple acts of feeding him, letting him out onto our garden, and cleaning up after him felt like a rebirth for me. He was happy again, snuggling next to me in bed for a full night of sleep every day, no longer playing the worried watchdog for his sick mistress. He was playful and loving, grateful for the little things. I starting calling him my sober dog, and I still do.

So when potential residents at my sober house started asking me if they could bring their pets to live there, I was conflicted. Stacy was the first woman to broach the subject.

"I need my little dog to live with me," she told me on the phone while I was interviewing her at rehab. She was on speakerphone with her discharge planner.

"What kind of dog do you have?" *Do I really want a dog at the sober house? I'm just starting to figure out how to handle the women.*

"Oh, she's an adorable little mutt. Her name is Pretzel." Stacy laughed, as if sharing a silly joke. Stacy was fifty-five years old and had been trying to get clean for over twenty years.

"Where is Pretzel now?" I asked.

"She's being boarded, but I really want her with me. She's the only thing I have left."

"I have a wonderful woman named Britt who lives near the house, and she watches my dogs when I'm out of town. Maybe she can watch Pretzel when you first move in, and you can have visits with her whenever you want."

"I would rather have her with me," Stacy said, sounding like a young child.

"I understand that," I told her, "but let's see how you do first, and if you are staying sober and complying with every-thing, Pretzel can come over for a weekend visit, and we'll see how she does…and how the other residents feel about her."

Stacy was happy with this compromise. She moved in, and her eighty-something-year-old mother took on Pretzel's rent in addition to Stacy's. Stacy's mother had been enabling Stacy for her entire life.

Pretzel came over for a visit one weekend after Stacy had lived with us for a month. Stacy promised that Pretzel was well behaved and house-trained and that she would sleep in her bed during her visit.

I came over unannounced the morning after Pretzel's overnight. I walked into the house at 10:00 a.m., and Pretzel began barking uncontrollably.

"Hi, Pretzel," I said, bending down to pet her. Pretzel squatted down immediately, peeing all over the living room floor. She was a mangy-looking little dog and was running around in circles like a spinning top. *She's a lot like Stacy*, I realized. *It really is true that dogs and owners are often very similar.* Stacy was manic at times, and Pretzel seemed to have taken her owner's mania on.

"Stacy!" I called out. "Where are you?"

"Just a minute," she replied. "I'm peeing."

So is your dog.

Stacy came out of her bedroom suite with a giddy smile on her face. She was wearing pajamas with dogs printed on them and pink furry slippers. She looked like a crazy grand-mother wearing children's clothing.

"Hi, Mal!" she said happily, running over to give me a hug. "Thank you so much for letting Pretzel sleep over. Everyone loves her." One of her roommates looked at me and rolled her eyes, insinuating otherwise.

"Stacy," I said firmly, "Pretzel just peed all over the floor." I pointed to the not-insignificant puddle, which was making its way across the living room floor, inching toward the rug. "Please clean it up right now."

"Oh, Pretzel!" Stacy said, laughing. "You're such a silly girl."

"I thought you said she was house-trained."

"Well, she almost is. Right, Pretzel? I think she was just so excited to see you."

Pretzel was still running around the living room, barking loudly. I tried to pick her up, but she was too pumped up to stay still.

I went into Stacy's room, and there was a wee-wee pad on the floor. A small poop sat in the center of it. "Stacy!" I called out again. "Please come in here and clean up this poop. This is unsanitary and not fair to your roommates."

Stacy came in and folded up the wee-wee pad and began walking toward the kitchen.

"What are you doing with that?"

"I'm going to put it in the trash."

"Kitchen trash is not for wee-wee pads, pee, and poop." I felt like I was speaking to a young child who had just gotten a puppy for the first time. "Flush the poop down the toilet and wrap the wee-wee pad and dirty paper towels with the pee on them into a plastic bag, and please throw it in the outdoor trash can."

"Okay," Stacy said, smiling. "Come on, Pretzel!" she sang out. Pretzel ignored her.

Clearly Pretzel was not going to be our first permanent housedog. I did allow Stacy to have Pretzel visit overnight many times over the months that she lived with us, but she was not fit for full-time residence.

Stacy did not remain sober and was asked to leave The Frog Pad twice due to relapse. Pretzel has been living with my dog sitter Britt for over two years now. Stacy goes in and out of detoxes and treatment centers. She has lived in many of the women's sober houses in the area, and none of them have allowed her to house Pretzel. She visits

Pretzel in between relapses, still holding on to the last thing she has.

Ashley was next. "My dog is in Pennsylvania, and I really want him to come down here. My ex-boyfriend has been watching him since I went to rehab, and he wants me to take him back." Ashley was working at a vet's office near the house. She had been sober for almost nine months.

"Can you take him to work with you every day?" I asked. The dog was a big bulldog, and I didn't want him alone at the house five days a week while Ashley worked eight to ten hours.

"Yes, I can," she promised. "He will be 100 percent my responsibility. His name is Roxy. Look how cute he is." She showed me a picture on her phone. I didn't think he was cute at all. He was big and fat, with an underbite.

Her ex drove the dog down from Pennsylvania. Roxy was huge, and he drooled and wheezed all the time. Ashley lived upstairs, and the entire floor housed three women. Both of her roommates had agreed to the dog moving in.

Giant bulldogs are not my favorite breed, but I wasn't going to be living with him.

A few days after Roxy moved in, I was giving a house tour. I walked upstairs with the prospective resident and heard barking coming from the bedroom. I opened the door carefully, and the dog's barking changed to growling.

"There's a dog living up here," I told the startled-looking woman with me, "but he's supposed to be at work with his owner."

The bedroom was a complete disaster. Roxy was perched on top of the middle bed (not Ashley's bed), barking and growling at us. He was baring his teeth, and drool was dripping from his mouth.

"Quiet, Roxy!" I commanded.

All the pillows in the room were scattered on the floor. The beautiful gray and white comforters I had so carefully chosen were covered with dog hair and dog spittle. I showed the woman the closets and bathroom quickly, closing Roxy back inside.

Ashley, I texted after my tour was over. *Why is Roxy alone at the house?*

I took him to work with me the first day, and he had terrible anxiety. I can't bring him anymore.

This wasn't what I agreed to.

There's nothing I can do. I paid my ex-boyfriend $500 to drive him down, and I can't afford a dog sitter.

We were stuck with Roxy for three months before Ashley moved out and got an apartment of her own.

"I have a parrot," a woman named Dina announced when I spoke to her from her inpatient treatment center.

I hadn't had a request for a bird before. *Birdcages can be really stinky. And birds can be super noisy.*

"He's staying at a pet spa now," Dina explained, "but I really can't live without him. His name is Fuzzy."

"I can't approve a bird moving in right away," I explained. "Typically, a woman moves in first, without her pet. If she is compliant for a period of time, she can then present her pet to the other residents in her house, and they decide whether or not to approve it.

Fuzzy and Dina had traveled all around the state of Florida in Dina's car for the past three years, while Dina smoked crystal meth. Dina had an ex-husband who was a semi-famous musician, and she had been well compensated when they divorced. From what her case manager and ex-husband told me before Dina moved in, she needed very long-term sober living. This last drug run had cost Dina her career, home, family, and friends. All she had left was Fuzzy.

I picked Dina up at treatment to take her over to The Frog Pad 2, where she would be living.

"We have to pick up Fuzzy now!" she announced about two minutes after I pulled out of the center. "It's not too far from here."

"I told you that you can't bring the bird to the house right away," I reminded her.

"It's so expensive at the pet spa here. Let's pick him up, and maybe I can find someplace less expensive for him near your house."

Nice try, and so not happening.

"Oh, dear God!" Dina almost shouted, "I miss my Fuzzy so badly!"

What kind of a relationship can a woman have with a bird? Does one even bond with a bird? It's not like you can cozy up with it.

Dina was fifty-seven years old and had lived a very successful and interesting life before crystal meth entered the picture. She had short, spiky black hair and very white skin. The remnants of beauty showed on her face. She was dressed in all black—half biker chick, the other half an artist. She had style for sure and was interesting company on the ride to the sober house. She had been raised in Germany, and her accent was still prominent.

After we completed her intake and my house manager Rita had come over to take her grocery shopping, I told Dina to relax for the rest of the evening and get herself settled in. We would pick her up in the morning for a women's meeting.

"Dina's not home," one of her roommates told me later that night when I stopped by to see how she was doing. "She went to visit her bird."

What? I had clearly told her to stay home until the next morning.

"She took an Uber." The pet spa was a forty-minute drive from the sober house. I couldn't believe that she had done this.

Dina, I texted her. *I asked you to stay home and relax and unpack tonight. You can't just take Uber without asking my permission.*

I had to see Fuzzy.

You cannot visit him again without my permission. You need to settle in, focus on your recovery, and get to know your housemates.

Sorry. It won't happen again.

Two days later, while Rita was doing bed and chore checks, one of Dina's housemates told Rita that Fuzzy had slept over the night before. Rita called me immediately.

"What? I told her that bird could not come over for at least a month. She hasn't even signed up for an IOP intake yet."

"I know," Rita said.

"Where is she now?"

"I don't know," she said. "There's a little birdcage in her room, but no bird, and Dina isn't here."

Where are you, Dina? I texted. *I told you that your bird could not come to the house, and I understand that he slept over last night.*

I couldn't help it. I went to visit him, and I've missed him so much.

He is not allowed in the house.

Rita and I went over to meet with Dina that afternoon. She was packing her bags—the same ones that she had just unpacked three days earlier.

"Where are you going?" I asked.

"I'm going to get Fuzzy. I can't stay in a house that won't allow me to have him."

"I was very clear before you moved in that you couldn't bring him right away, if at all. And what are you going to do? Your ex told me that you have no access to money."

"Well, he's wrong. I do have money. I have accounts he doesn't know about.

She called an Uber and began lugging her bags out to the driveway. She had so much matching luggage that it looked like she was going on a trip around the world, rather than to a pet spa to pick up her parrot.

"How are you going to get around with your bird and all these bags?" Rita asked her.

"That's not your concern," Dina replied, still wheeling bags through the living room.

"It is our concern though," I told her. "You came here because you wanted to get your life together. You've only been out of treatment for three days and haven't even started an IOP or had a meds evaluation. Why don't you stay a month since its already paid for and see how you feel then?"

Leaving before a resident had stayed for at least a month meant that she would lose her security deposit and the whole month's rent. I also had a concern that her medications were *off*, which could have been adding to her impulsive behavior.

"Not without Fuzzy."

"This is your disease speaking. It wants you to leave so that you won't have any accountability. Do you want to end up smoking crystal meth again?"

"Get out of my way!" she said, pushing past us.

I called her ex and told him what was going on.

"She doesn't have any money," he said.

"That's not what she says."

"Well, she's an adult. She can do whatever she wants. She's not my problem anymore."

He seemed like a nice guy the several times we had spoken, but he had detached from her when he realized that she wasn't willing to get the help she needed. Normally he had his staff deal with her. He had a few people who managed all of his affairs, and they were the ones who usually dealt with her since she called incessantly.

"It seems like you're the only person she has left," I reminded him.

"She only calls me to manipulate money from me. I told her that if she doesn't stay at your house, I wouldn't give her any more money. Oh, and be careful," he added, "I think she has a few guns with her."

"What? How is that possible? I picked her up directly from treatment."

"I'm just telling you. She told me she has three guns."

Dina's Uber pulled up, and the driver began to pile her bags into his big SUV.

"Thank you for everything!" Dina said, throwing her arms around me and giving me a hug.

I called her treatment center and let them know what had happened. I had covered all my bases, but I was sad that Dina hadn't been willing to give sober living a real try.

Dina sent me a text about a month later. *Hello from Germany! Fuzzy and I are doing well. Miss you!*

Miss you too, I wrote back.

As I was leaving an early morning meeting at Crossroads one day, someone called out my name. It was Leah, a beautiful young woman who had been in and out of recovery for many years. For the past several months, she had been sharing from the heart, and it seemed like she was finally ready to stay sober and work a thorough recovery program.

"I know this is a strange question," she began, "but I'm getting out of treatment in a few days, and I have no money and a two-hundred-pound dog. We're going to be homeless. I know you have sober houses." Her beautiful blue eyes filled up with tears.

Here we go again, but this one has no money at all, and the biggest dog ever.

"Let me think about it, Leah." My initial thought was *No way*.

As I sat quietly later that morning, my heart began to open. *Maybe I do want Leah and her two-hundred-pound dog,* I realized. *What a wonderful thing it would be to help her since she seems so willing this time. Maybe I can help save her life.*

What kind of dog do you have? I asked via text.

He's a St. Bernard. I'll send you a pic.

She immediately sent a picture over. He looked very big and sloppy. *His name is Bernie. He's a big sweetheart.*

Let's talk about it in person.

Sure! Thank you.

"Where's the dog now?" I asked her over a coffee at Starbucks the next morning. I had taken her out on pass from her treatment center.

"He's with my ex-boyfriend, but he won't keep him once I graduate from treatment. He has been watching Bernie for three months."

"Every time I bring someone in on a scholarship, or even a partial scholarship, she ends up taking advantage of me and leaving on very bad terms. I like to think that I'm doing this work for a reason, and that somebody with no money would be especially grateful, but that has not been my experience so far."

"I promise that I'll make you proud if you give me a chance," she said, her eyes filling up with tears again. "Nobody will take me and Bernie in, and I don't know what to do. I got treatment totally for free this time, and I am so grateful. I'll do anything to pay you back."

Leah had a job lined up and promised to begin paying me as much as she could as soon as she was getting a paycheck. *With the size of her dog, I doubted there would be much money left after feeding him.*

"I'm going to break the mold," she promised me. "If you give me this chance, I will be forever grateful."

I brought Leah and Bernie up at the house meeting that Friday. "Who would be okay with a two-hundred-pound dog moving in?" I asked my women.

"What kind of dog is it?" one of the residents asked, sounding excited.

"He's a St. Bernard. Here's a picture." I passed my cell phone around with the photo that Leah had sent me. The women seemed extremely excited.

"He would be at House Two," I told them. "So who wants him?"

One hand shot up, and then another and another. The women who hadn't raised their hands looked around the room, and more and more hands shot up. Finally, there were sixteen raised hands—it was unanimous.

"Okay, then," I said, "I'll let you know when they're moving in."

Leah and Bernie moved in a few days later. *Oh my god—he's as big as a small horse!* I thought when I went over to do her intake.

"I'm forever grateful to you, Mallory," Leah told me, her blue eyes tearing up. "I don't know what we would have done if you hadn't taken us in."

"Just make me proud," I told her, giving her a big hug, "and don't pick up a drink."

Within three days I realized that Leah was a drama queen and a master manipulator. Everything was about her—twenty-four hours a day. She sucked the air out of a room and talked about herself constantly. The dog was just a prop that she used to get attention.

"Leah," I told her, "you need to focus on your recovery, your job, and taking care of Bernie. Every time I see you, you're crying. Where is the gratitude that we spoke of?"

"I'm emotional," she cried. "Why are you bullying me? Now you're just making me more upset. You're making me want to drink."

"I'm not making you anything, Leah. I'm telling you what you need to hear, not what you want to hear. That isn't always easy."

Leah began gossiping about me to the other women in the houses. She told them that I was a bully and that I was using her as my punching bag. Meanwhile, Bernie was destroying her bedroom. He would climb onto all the beds and make himself comfortable. The beds were full-size, but he was so gigantic that they looked like little dog beds when he jumped onto them. He was filthy, and the three beds in her room were quickly stained and dirty. Leah was too busy to clean them.

"I'm trying to make a living," she cried to me. "Bernie has no food, and his dog food is super expensive."

So why did you get a two-hundred-pound dog?

"He's ruining all the bedding in your room. Why can't your ex watch him again?"

"He's mad at me," she cried.

Leah was such a beautiful girl. Her skin was porcelain, she had a little dancer's body, and her crying blue eyes were stunning. When I first met her, she reminded me of a young Elizabeth Taylor. Before long, I couldn't stand to look at her. Her eyes were always full of tears. *She would be so pretty if she would just laugh,* I realized.

It was impossible to turn Leah's attitude around. She played the poor victim, and if I tried to get her into gratitude, or reality, she would burst into tears and say that I was bullying her again.

"Leah, you're never going to be happy if you don't start taking ahold of your own life. You have an Ivy League education—you can be whatever you want to be if you just don't pick up a drink." She was working as a cashier at a burger joint about twenty hours a week, bringing home less than two hundred dollars after taxes.

"I don't know what I want to be," she said. "Maybe I should get my PhD and be a therapist."

Great idea. Another five years of schooling, with no money coming in, and another crazy therapist out there who can't manage her own life.

"You're thirty-five years old," I reminded her. "Maybe for right now you need to just focus on making some good money so you can pay for your own food and rent. You could get a job with medical insurance." She had been doing the recovery dance for over ten years, never staying sober for more than a few months at a time.

"Mallory's such a bitch," she told her roommate later that day. "She thinks she's so helpful and spiritual, but all she does is beat the shit out of me."

When her roommate shared this with me, I realized again just how sick Leah was. I had made a huge mistake by bringing her in. She was a complete narcissist, and playing the victim was her forte.

I had been the only person willing to bring her and her two-hundred-pound dog into my house, and she was unable to use this free time to work on her recovery and her career. Instead, she found another guy, a heroin addict with a few months sober. She found him at her IOP, and an immediate romance developed.

"He's the love of my life," she told anyone who would listen. "He's going to take care of me."

Relapse, treatment, man. Relapse, treatment, man. Relapse, treatment, man, and dog. Leah had done this dance for a very long time. She moved out after three months, leaving her ruined bedding unwashed. She didn't say goodbye or thank you.

Within a few weeks of Leah leaving and moving in with her boyfriend, he started shooting dope again. Apparently

Leah wasn't enough to keep him sober. Leah continues to badmouth me to anyone who will listen. She hasn't worked a day in six months, and he is back in treatment. I pray for her often: *Please give Leah everything she wants and needs today. Amen.*

We have had many more dogs than I have talked about here, and some of them were even well behaved and taken care of almost entirely by their rightful owners. We have a baby tortoise, and he has been with us for over six months. He has grown from a tiny little thing into a healthy specimen. He lives in a huge wooden crate with a sunlamp shining down on him. One of our residents has even built him a beautiful outdoor sunning garden, and he enjoys bathing there often.

Feral cats have been an ongoing problem for us. Many of my women find themselves unable to resist feeding them, and there have been times where our driveways are crawling with cats and kittens. Unfortunately, many of them are born with terrible diseases, and we have had to call animal control many times to have them taken away. We have rented safe traps to try and catch and then spay and neuter some of these cats, but they are pretty good at snatching food and then running away. I find that just not feeding them works best. We can love them from across the street. Unfortunately, I still find bowls outside both of my houses, filled with cat food and water. Usually I just let it go.

The Frog Pad One sits on a canal, which is teeming with wildlife. We have ducks, turtles, iguanas, fish, wild birds, and frogs. I frequently stop by and find my residents laughing as they feed these animals. Many of them have been given names. These animals are the most perfect of all for newly sober women.

It is often said in the rooms of Alcoholics Anonymous that we should stay out of relationships for the first year. Many people with long-term recovery also believe that pets are too much for a newly sober person also. We are told to try taking care of a plant first. My houses are full of plants, and many of them are thriving.

Don't You Want to Make
Some *Real* Money?

Delray Beach was always my safe and happy place. I didn't have a coke connection there, so whenever I visited, I felt healthy and happy. I could dine and drink on Atlantic Avenue without worrying about calling my dealer and ending up high again. The beach, early morning runs, tennis, and yoga were not conducive to drug use, and I was grateful that I didn't have a connection there.

Little did I know that Delray Beach was informally called *The Recovery Capital of America,* and when I got sober, I was shocked to find that there were literally hundreds of 12-step meetings in the area every week. There was a sunrise beach meeting right near our house on weekends. I would carry my beach chair over, watching the sunrise, amazed by the beauty of life and my own sobriety. During season, the circle of people holding hands at the end of the meeting was vast, and I knew for sure that I wasn't alone. Crossroads Club held meetings from 7:00 a.m. until 10:00

p.m. Many of the meetings I began to attend had fifty to a hundred and fifty people in attendance. It was comforting to realize that I was living among other people in recovery, and I began to collect phone numbers and developed relationships with some of them.

"You're so popular!" my eighty-year-old mother-in-law said to me one day when we were having lunch together in town. People from the meetings would say hello to me by name, and it hadn't gone unnoticed. "How do you know all these people?"

"They're my friends," I said.

"You're amazing," she told me with a smile.

When I first started talking about opening my sober house, an older man named Johnny from the 7:00 a.m. meeting asked me to have breakfast with him. He was over twenty-five years sober, and I respected his program. He was well known and seemed to help a lot of newcomers.

"You know," he began, "I'm opening an IOP." He elaborated on his big plans for treatment and a drug lab. "If you refer your women to my IOP and lab, you can make some *real* money."

"What do you mean?"

"We'll pay you the big bucks for your referrals," he said, his mouth full of eggs and toast. *This guy is a pig,* I thought, looking at the food gathering at the corners of his lips.

I called my sober house mentor and told him about my conversation.

"That's completely illegal," he confirmed. "That guy is going to charge big bucks to insurance companies for IOP and drug testing. He's offering you kickbacks for your referrals."

I was disgusted. My father had always taught me that referrals in business were strictly for companies that did good work and never for personal gain. This was a wonderful gift that he instilled in all of us growing up, and I had never wavered from his advice on this matter. I definitely didn't heed all of his warnings—especially when it came to drinking, drugging, and men—but I was clear on business ethics. I hired my own drug lab and paid for my residents to UA out of the money I got for rent. Johnny went on to make a lot of money, but he kept running into walls as insurance companies changed their laws, and he recently moved to Europe when he realized that the well here had run dry for him. He's looking to make some big money overseas.

The media has gone wild down here, reporting on the money billed to insurance companies for UAs over the past several years. One man was just arrested for billing over $58 million over the course of less than five years. He allegedly paid someone to scout for insured addicts in the Delray Beach area so he could charge their insurance companies money for inferior treatment programs and drug screens. It worked for a while, and it is reported that he boasted of his success on his Facebook page, holding piles of money and sporting expensive jewelry and fast cars—a recovering addict, grateful to be sober, but seeing the opportunities for real money. He has been released on a $250,000 bond and awaits trial. His "junkie hunter," as the press alludes to him, is in prison awaiting trial, unable to post his own $200,000 bond.

There are many stories on television and in the news-papers about overdoses and deaths in and around Delray Beach, but none about people who are recovering and running certified and ethical sober homes and treatment centers. I confronted a local reporter at a sober fellowship recently and asked her why she only writes about people who are dying and facilities that are unethical, rather than balancing her reporting with stories of hope. Why wasn't she directing people to go to facilities that are properly licensed and doing good work? To paraphrase, her answer was that it is too difficult to vet the good facilities, resources are low, and the public wants to hear the negative news rather than the positive.

After these articles were published, my phone did not ring for over three weeks with people looking for a FARR approved house for women. I didn't receive a single phone call or give even one tour to a prospective resident. The calls that I did get during this time were from IOPs who were all suffering from lower numbers of patients, hoping to get referrals from my houses (not with kickbacks!). Not a single new resident moved in for almost two months after articles in the *New York Times* published on June 20, 2017, and the *Palm Beach Post* around the same time began slamming our reputation. Typically, I receive between one and three phone calls a day for my sober homes, which have a total of seventeen beds, and three is not uncommon—receiving no calls for weeks is extremely rare. The media was definitely having a negative impact on my business.

On June 25, 2017, Delray Beach mayor Cary Glickstein closed a *Sunday Night with Megyn Kelly* interview by saying, "Keep them closer to home. They're not getting better in South Florida." The entire story told of women who had been sent down here to get sober, only to die at the hands of unethical treatment and sober living facilities. Who would want to send their loved ones here if this is all people hear?

"I might as well just close down House Two," I told Mark sadly when I heard our mayor telling people to stay away. "Who's going to come here now?"

"It will blow over," Mark assured me. "And when the unethical houses close down, there will be more women needing houses like yours."

Palm Beach County's state attorney Dave Aronberg also appeared on this show, talking about the "total scam" surrounding sober homes in our county, which includes West Palm Beach, Lake Worth, Delray Beach, Boynton Beach, and Boca Raton. There was absolutely no mention of a single person getting sober down here and saving his or her life, and the numbers of recovering addicts and alcoholics here are staggering.

Megyn Kelly went on to report on a sober home opera-
tor in Boynton Beach who is serving twenty-seven years in
Federal prison. He and his wife were giving drugs to addicts
in their so-called sober homes and even prostituting their
residents. They were patient brokering and holding people
with insurance hostage in order to prevent them from leaving with their coveted insurance cards.

My houses don't involve insurance. My residents are all
self-pay. Every service offered by us is covered in a woman's rent. If my residents need IOP or private therapists, I
refer them to respected rehabs and professionals, because
I know they will be cared for and treated in their best interests. The people and places that I refer to answer my phone
calls and are available to discuss our shared clients, and all
my residents sign waivers allowing their treatment teams to
speak to me. I am on the phone with them often.

The fact that the press does nothing to validate the truth
that there are sober homes and treatment centers in South
Florida that are working to save their loved ones is disgrace-
ful. These problems and issues are not pandemic to our
area, but we have become a target, and Aronberg stated in
his interview that "this is a case where most of the apples

are spoiled." What I didn't understand is why Aronberg, Glickstein, and Kelly didn't say a single word about the houses that are FARR certified and have FCB licensing as well. People are still coming to South Florida to get sober, so why not point them in the right direction?

In late 2015 I got a call from my friend Melena. I originally met her at the 7:00 a.m. meeting at Crossroads and then bumped into her at an early morning in Soho. We became fast friends. Melena is one of those young women who came to South Florida years ago to get sober. She went to treatment and lived in a sober house. She has been sober ever since and has a beautiful life. She lives in Manhattan but visits Florida several times a year.

"My dad's opening a drug lab in Florida," she told me. "He wants me to help him." Melena's dad lives in Boca, and he is not in recovery. He's a successful businessman. "He wants me to help him sign sober houses and IOPs up for him." She sounded excited.

"That sounds very shady," I warned her. "I buy my own UAs and do them myself."

"Yes, but his lab will pay you for each UA that he processes."

"Stay away," I told her. "We can discuss it more when I see you, but this is a gray area and is for people who are just trying to make a lot of money off insurance companies."

Melena stayed away, but her father didn't. He was arrested in May 2017 for five counts of patient brokering. His two partners were also arrested. Between the two of them, they had earned two million dollars in a six-month period. Fast cash, but they are both facing prison if convicted. One of the men who brought them patients with insurance from three sober homes for urine testing was paid one hundred and fifty thousand dollars up front by the team.

There is a couple I met in the rooms of A.A. They talk a good program. The husband Danny owns an IOP in Delray Beach, and a woman named Marsha who moved into The Frog Pad chose to go there. Within a month, he had moved her over to his new sober house and made her his house manager. She had excellent insurance. His wife was her sponsor, and she had only three months of sobriety. I was flabbergasted by the unprofessionalism of this. Within a week, she had convinced another one of my residents, Cathy, to move over there, and this woman was given free rent in exchange for using her insurance money to pay for IOP and drug testing there. Then a third resident of mine named Naomi decided to go to IOP there, though she remained at my sober living home.

"Some weird stuff is going on over there," Naomi told me.

"Like what?"

"A lot of people are getting high, and Danny doesn't care."

"What do you mean he doesn't care?"

"He just lets them stay there and continue going to IOP."

Before long, Naomi had relapsed with some of the people in her IOP group. I went in to speak to Danny. I had just found out that Marsha had relapsed too.

"You should move some more of your women to my IOP," he told me, puffing away at a gigantic vapor cigarette.

"Why's that?"

"We really treat the root causes," he gloated. "I was sober for over ten years, and then I relapsed on crack. It was really bad. I lost everything, but I can always make a lot of money."

He went on and on, boasting about all of his successes and losses, bragging about his education and how he had learned to stay sober this time through intensive therapy. *Isn't that what most treatment centers do? I didn't see what makes him or his place so special.*

"I pay for my patients to have dinner together every night," he continued. "Last year I spent over two hundred grand on dinners. My accountant was so angry about this, but I think it's great to feed them all together."

Two hundred thousand dollars was just a fraction of what Danny was billing insurance for IOP and UAs. His patients never left IOP, and I saw some of them following him into meetings a year after they had started with him. Most IOPs ran for two months. As long as Danny's patients kept relapsing, their insurance would cover more treatment. I was disgusted and vowed never to work with anyone from his IOP again. This was a clear case of supposed *sober* people taking complete advantage of people who were trying to save their lives.

Cathy called and asked me to meet with her. She expressed her concerns about her IOP.

"Danny's charging my insurance fifteen hundred dollars a day for IOP, and last week we spent one day at a water park, one day watching a movie together in a treatment room, and the next day he offered us bowling, but I didn't even go."

"Why didn't they have groups and individual therapy?" I asked.

"Two of the staff were out sick, so he didn't have anyone to run them."

I just shook my head in disbelief.

"And Marsha is drinking again," she said. "She keeps going to her apartment in Palm Beach and relapsing. Danny says my insurance sucks, and he wants to kick me out."

Cathy moved back to my house shortly after, where I gave her a partial scholarship.

Danny's company continues to move locations and change names. This is often an indication of an owner running from the law. They change their programs to stay ahead of the law, hoping to continue raking in huge profits at the expense of providing caring professional services. When Danny or his wife are chosen to speak at an A.A. meeting that I'm at, I make an immediate beeline for the bathroom, or go to the lobby to buy a bottle of cold water. *Bless them, change me,* I pray silently.

Want to make some *real* money? I remembered being asked several times. People thought I was crazy for steering away, but I had been forewarned about bad operators, and my goal in opening my sober homes was not to get rich quickly. Call me crazy if you want, but I am actually trying to help women learn how to live sober lives like I have been taught. At least I can put my head down on my pillow each night with a clear conscience. I'm not getting rich, but I'm also not tossing and turning with fears of being the next person to be arrested. To me, there is no comparison.

There are some bad apples down here in South Florida for sure, but they exist all over the country. South Florida is not the only place where people are dying and overdosing in large numbers. I say that the media should report on the good apples too, because there are a lot of people down here trying to stay alive.

Not Now, I'm Doing Yoga

When I was forty years old, I was running a lot—training for and completing marathons—and I was always aching. My body was so stiff that I couldn't even bend down and touch my toes. One of my friends suggested that I try yoga as a way to stretch out and counterbalance all the pounding that my body was taking. It wasn't until I reached the end of my active addiction that yoga really started to soothe me. I found myself crying quietly at the end of class sometimes, lying in *shavasana*, which is the resting pose at the end of class, often a meditation.

Whenever I visited Delray Beach, my friend Lorrie and I would go to a *vinyasa* yoga class taught by a man named Seth on Sundays at a downtown hotel. Mark would join us too when he entered my life. Seth's class had live music and was in a big ballroom in this beautiful deco hotel that was built in the 1920s. As many as a hundred people practice there on Sundays, possibly even more—people of all ages, shapes, genders, sizes, and levels.

I had a yoga practice in Tribeca too, but my teacher there was a much-harsher critic. Elsa was a young, beautiful blonde, but she seemed to have it in for me.

"Everyone line up for headstands," she would direct. "Except Mallory. Mallory, you can stay in child's pose on your mat."

What? Why can't I try a headstand too? I want to go upside down.

"Breathe through your nose," Elsa would tell the class. "Except Mallory."

It was true that I often couldn't breathe through my nose. Cocaine had me stuffed up a lot of the time, though I attributed my stuffiness to allergies.

Seth never made me feel less than. "If you're sitting on your mat and breathing through your nose," he told the class, "you're doing yoga.

"If you see someone doing something you wished that you could do, just close your eyes and imagine yourself doing it. You will get all the benefits that the person who is doing it gets.

"When I first started doing yoga," he would say, "I sucked so bad, but I felt so good. I couldn't figure out why I loved something that I sucked at, but I kept doing it."

I totally related to this. I definitely sucked at yoga, but when I got sober, I started to love it. Seth's class was healing and restorative.

"If you're thinking about anything other than doing yoga," he would say, "just tell yourself—not now, I'm doing yoga."

This cracked me up, because I was almost always thinking about something other than yoga when he said this. *What should I have for lunch? What meeting should I go to today? I really should go to Publix and buy groceries so I can cook a nice, healthy meal tonight. I need to remember to call my hairdresser and schedule an appointment to get my roots dyed.*

"Not now, I'm doing yoga." As soon as Seth said these words, I cleared my mind of thoughts from yesterday or thoughts of later today.

"Spread your fingers wide," Seth said. "Make little teepees with your fingers."

I focused my attention back to my mat and my not-so-imperfect practice.

Back in New York, in Elsa's class, I heard Seth's voice in my head. I was perfect just the way I was. I was alive and sober, practicing yoga. Mindfulness, or staying in the moment, was a big part of the A.A. program, and yoga was helping me to achieve this.

On Tuesday evenings at Seth's other yoga studio, he facilitated a yoga *nidra* meditation at the end of his class. For about twenty minutes, he guided us through a closed-eye visualization. My mind began to open up in these meditations, my brain entering a fourth dimension. Seth told us that twenty minutes of yoga nidra meditation were the equivalent of five to six hours of sleep. I would float off into bliss while Mark snored softly beside me.

"Seth," I said to him after class, "thank you so much. You're changing my life."

He put his big, muscular arms around me and hugged me close.

"I know," he said, looking at me with his wise blue eyes. "I know." I felt like he did know. He had a gift, and it was helping me heal. Sometimes I looked around his classes at people doing scorpion poses, and crows, and amazing handstands. I closed my eyes and imagined myself doing exactly what they were doing.

"This is time-released yoga," he would say. The high was real—and it was healthy. As tired as the classes made me physically, my mind was clear and alert for hours when I rolled up my mat and walked away.

I started inviting Seth to practice yoga *nidra* meditation at The Frog Pad shortly after I opened. Many of my women would not venture out to his classes on Sunday and Tuesday, even though I paid for them. If I brought him into my houses during our Friday morning meetings, though, they had to participate. I also started bringing his wife Cari and other gifted teachers from his studio into the houses to practice with us. Some of the women who were too out of shape or unmotivated to go to their outside classes began to participate. Quite a few of them started accompanying me to the Colony after that, and to Buddha Lounge, and some joined up for teacher training. For some of them it has been life changing, as it was for me.

Opening the sober house robbed me of my freedom. For many long months, I did everything myself. If I didn't know how to do everything myself, I didn't feel that I would be capable of training someone to assist me. And money was an issue too—a great deal of my savings had gone into opening, and I didn't have enough residents to justify hiring anyone. Taxes, property management, insurance, power, supplies, drug tests, Breathalyzers, yoga classes—the list of expenses was very long. I wasn't trying to get rich, but I didn't want to blow the remains of a lifetime of work either.

My daily activities were vast. I drove residents to 12-step meetings, performed morning bed checks, and made sure that chores were completed. Medications had to be unlocked, dispensed, and then locked up again. My residents needed rides to the supermarket and the pharmacy regularly. House supplies needed to be purchased. If anyone needed to see a doctor or a dentist for an illness or procedure, I accompanied them. Random UAs had to be done. Tours and interviews needed to be conducted for potential residents. Fellowship was important too, so I developed Tacos and Tattoos, buying and helping prepare a buffet-style healthy dinner, and bringing Flash Tats over and helping my women choose and affix them. Preparation for, and the running of, house meetings were essential, as were one-on-ones with each of my residents on a regular basis. I had to call and visit treatment centers, marketing for potential clients. If the discharge planners and therapists didn't know that my house existed or what I was offering, they would be unlikely to refer any clients to me.

My phone rang constantly with calls from residents, their families, and their therapists. There were services to be booked and coordinated, including career counseling, housekeeping, nutrition, yoga, Thai massage, reflexology, and meditation. Things were constantly in need of repair, so I had a list of handymen on call and needed to notify residents with a "Man Alert" whenever they were heading our way. And at the end of an already very long day, I had to do bed checks at night and Breathalyze all the residents.

On top of being exhausted, I was stressed out a lot. If anything was reported to me, I had to go over immediately to investigate. These situations ranged from someone suspecting another woman of being "on" something, to somebody calling me crying because another resident had "bullied" her. My phone beeped incessantly with texts and calls.

Socializing was difficult. Shortly after opening House One, Mark and I had dinner with another couple. My phone kept beeping with texts, which I would quickly read and then respond to if they pertained to the house.

"Why don't you just put that damn phone away?" the husband that we were out with asked with irritation.

"It's work," I said.

"You can't even have a bloody meal without working? What kind of a life is that? Do you think that's fair to Mark?"

I placed my phone on my lap, where I could self-consciously glance at it secretly. These women were my responsibility, and no social occasion was going to take that away. I continued to text as innocuously as possible throughout the rest of the meal, feeling like a child who was misbehaving.

On another evening out with friends, I received a frantic text from the house. I excused myself and went outside to call the resident and calm her down. Back inside, just a few minutes later, another call came in that I felt I had to take. We hadn't ordered yet, and I saw one of my friends looking at the other with irritation. Ignoring them, I went outside again. Mark came out a few minutes later, urging me to come back inside, or at least to give him my dinner order. I put my hand over the phone. "I'm talking to the parent of a potential resident," I whispered to him. "I need more women."

"They're really getting annoyed," he said. Mark was extremely understanding about my new venture, but he didn't like controversy and wanted everyone to be happy all the time.

"Fine," I continued, "I'll leave. You can stay with them." I stormed through the parking lot, getting back to my phone call and away from these unwanted interruptions. "They can drive you home," I continued, "or you can take an Uber."

It was amazing to me that my friends didn't understand how seriously I was taking my new business. If they couldn't bear with me, then I figured they really weren't good friends. In retrospect, I realize that maybe I should have just stayed home, fielding my work in private. At that time, though, I was trying to balance my life, and Mark loved to socialize. He had already lived through me giving up alcohol—it didn't seem fair that he should have to give up evenings out with friends too.

Most Sunday mornings, after completing my ninety-minute yoga class, my phone has twenty text messages and three voice mails awaiting my attention. I have learned enough to know that I can't take calls during yoga. I guess that could apply to meals as well, but I'm not there yet.

I have amazing staff now, which takes a load off, but I'm extremely hands-on, especially when it comes to relapses, behavioral issues, and family or therapist interactions. It isn't unusual for me to have to pause a television show, or an outing, to take a long-awaited call, leaving Mark, or one of my visiting children or friends, waiting patiently for me to finish.

In May of 2016, my friend Lorrie and I went to an ashram for a weekend yoga retreat with Seth and Cari and some other yogis. We were looking forward to two days and nights away together, which was something we had never done before. We left Delray Beach on Friday afternoon, and I had a relatively uninterrupted drive up and evening the first day. The next morning, while we were volunteering at a food drive, my phone rang and pinged constantly. One of the women was reported to be drinking, and I had to investigate. This involved speaking to her housemates, my house manager, the resident in question, as well as her mother and therapist. It took most of the day to resolve, and there was damage control with the other residents too.

The resident swore that the wine and bourbon bottles found in her property weren't hers.

"I'm not safe here!" she cried on the phone. "Why are people trying to sabotage me? I haven't been drinking!

People are planting bottles with my things!" All the evidence told me that she was lying, but she was Breathalyzing sober, so it was difficult to prove. "I don't even drink wine!" she continued. "When I drink, it's gin—straight out of the bottle. I wouldn't waste my money on wine!"

"Sorry," I said to Lorrie, after about fifteen phone calls.

She laughed. "Can't you tell them what Seth says?"

"What?"

"Not now. I'm doing yoga."

We both laughed.

"Actually," she said, "that's a good title for a chapter in your book."

I guess I agreed.

Sitting at my house meeting some Friday mornings, surrounded by beautiful women, I am overcome with a joy like I have never before experienced. These are my women. This is my sober house. Many of them are healing before my eyes. I'm still not sure how all this happened, but I am filled with a peace and serenity that I have never felt before at any time in my working life. My work and my life are finally totally seamless.

I often say that I had to finally cross over that line, into addiction, and then get sober, and work a daily recovery program, to find my true meaning and purpose in life. If I have helped one other person to stay sober, it has all been worth it. *Namaste*.

Ignorance Is Not Bliss

Right after Natalie moved into my house, her sponsor Cathi grabbed me after a morning meeting.

"You don't need to worry about Natalie," she told me. "She really isn't a drug addict."

"What do you mean?" Natalie had just finished seven months of inpatient treatment for opiates and benzos.

"She had a lot of surgeries," Cathi explained. "She was prescribed lots of stuff, and she couldn't get off on her own. She's totally fine now."

Cathi and I had come into the program at about the same time. Both of us were married to *normies*, we were close in age, and we were both moms. Cathi worked a great program and helped many women—sponsoring them, driving them to and from meetings, taking them out of treatment on passes for sober fun.

I quickly learned that Natalie was a major addict, just like most of us. She had been prescribed a lot of addictive medications, but she had chosen to continue taking them for years after she needed them. She was constantly seeing her psychiatrist, complaining of pain, anger issues, moodiness. She was what we call a *doctor shopper.* Her doctor was happy to provide her with medications that nobody in recovery should ever take. This doctor was affiliated with one of the largest treatment centers in Delray Beach, and I was shocked that he would prescribe these meds.

In recovery, we don't take medications that are mood or mind-altering. Alcohol is a drug. So is weed. As sober people, we are expected to manage our doctors and make the right choices. For so many people, including Natalie, as long as a doctor prescribes a medication, they rationalize taking it.

"He's a doctor, Mallory," Natalie told me when I explained that she could not have the medication that had just been prescribed to her. "You aren't."

"I know I'm not a doctor, Natalie, but in recovery we don't take benzos and opiates. You should know this after seven months in treatment and going to A.A. meetings every day. As addicts, we have lost the right to these drugs."

"But I need them," she told me. "Please just let me take one every day. I can't control my anger, and I don't want you to kick me out!"

"I'm not going to kick you out, honey. I'm going to teach you how to manage your anger without medication."

Natalie looked at me with her bright blue eyes. She had a little button nose and was batting her lashes at me, trying to look cute. Maybe she thought she could charm me into allowing her to take pills that weren't allowed in my houses, but she was wrong. When she began reaching out to me, telling me that she was raging inside, I talked her through it—teaching her to breathe, to pause, sit quietly.

After she celebrated a year sober, Natalie moved out and got her own apartment nearby. Without our structure and random UAs, she started doctor shopping within a very short time. Fewer meetings led to no meetings at all. She stopped meeting with Cathi. Natalie holed up in her apartment, taking pills and eventually drinking. A local urgent care was more than happy to feed her addiction with whatever she asked for—Ambien, Xanax, codeine, Demerol. This continued for over a year until she cried out for help, and I was finally able to assist her in getting into a detox and inpatient facility. She has been unwilling to attend groups so far or to meet with her individual therapist. Instead, she complains of terrible pain and insists on visiting the hospital, hoping for the relief that she wants so badly. She wants to leave as soon as possible, returning to her apartment and doing things her way. I'm afraid she will die there—alone and miserable.

"Natalie is *not* a drug addict, remember?" I kidded with Cathi last week.

"She had me fooled. That's for sure."

A regular at my women's meeting, Shelby approached me about sponsorship one day. A big woman, usually dressed in bright flowing garments, she shared about how she had gotten almost a year and a half sober, despite constant struggles with money and men.

"Would you be willing to sponsor me?" she asked me after a meeting one morning.

"Call me every day for a week and we'll see how it goes."

We found a time that worked for both of us, and Shelby began calling me.

The calls were not short. Shelby would start in right away, telling me about her job woes, the guy who was staying with her, and much more. These conversations were stream of consciousness on her part, and I tried to advise her when I could get a word in. On the fourth day, when I suggested that she might want to consider finding a thera-pist, she mentioned her prescription meds.

"What are you taking?"

"Xanax and Klonopin."

In A.A., these pills are not allowed. Shelby admitted to being on large doses of both.

"Shelby, you can't take benzos if you're sober. Xanax and Klonopin are both mood and mind-altering."

"They're both prescribed, so I can take them."

"Well, I don't sponsor women who take those. Some people will sponsor you if you smoke weed or take pills, but I don't believe in it."

Shelby's typically soft tone shifted to anger. "Well, you're a *fucking* judgmental bitch!" she yelled, disconnect-ing the call.

Shelby just picked up a three-year medallion. She con-tinues to brag about her recovery in the rooms and is now raising her hand when the group is asked who is willing to be a sponsor. There is no way that one of my residents would be allowed to work with her.

Bethany was one of my very first residents. From LA, she had been prescribed Adderall to help her concentration when she was studying for the SATs in high school. Fifteen years later, she was arrested for doctor shopping. Her tolerance became so high that she had purchased over ten thousand pills in a two-year period. The police thought she was dealing, but she wasn't. She had swallowed every single one of them herself.

Bethany slept whenever she wasn't in treatment. "I haven't slept in years," she told me one day, laughing. "I would stay up all night, cleaning my apartment." Now she was sleeping ten to twelve hours a night. One day she wasn't feeling well, and I took her to a nearby urgent care. She thought she might have strep throat.

"She's in recovery," I told the doctor and nurses as soon as we arrived. "Don't give her anything mood or mind-altering."

I entered the examining room with her and took a seat. After her exam, the doctor prescribed an antibiotic. As we were leaving the examination room, the nurse walked in and handed Bethany a pill and a cup of water. Bethany took the pill greedily into her hand and was about to swallow it.

"What is that?" I asked the nurse.

"Demerol."

"Did you not hear me telling you that this woman is in recovery? She cannot take that." I grabbed the pill from Bethany's hand and gave it back to the nurse. *What is wrong with these people? Are they completely naive about addiction and recovery? Didn't they learn about this stuff in nursing and medical school?*

Last October, I wasn't feeling well, and I went to the hospital. After some tests, I was told that my appendix had exploded inside me. "I'm in recovery," I told anyone who would listen. "I don't want any pain meds other than Tylenol."

I was petrified. For years I had listened to people in meetings explain that they had been sober and then had undergone surgery and been prescribed pain medication, ultimately leading to a new addiction. Even people who planned for others in recovery to dole out their meds often fell back into their disease, sometimes taking their friends along with them. I knew that pain couldn't kill me, but opiates could.

When I was put into a room after my surgery, the white board in front of my bed read "Dilaudid" in big letters. I was mortified. I didn't want people to see that on my board. I was sober, and I wasn't going to take opiates. I asked the nurse to erase the word from my board, but she refused. When my sponsor and other sober supports came to the hospital to visit me, I was quick to point out that I was not taking Dilaudid. Toradol (like strong Tylenol) was working just fine, thank you, and I wasn't going to become another relapse statistic.

When the pain became unbearable the second night, my surgeon insisted that I take a dose of Dilaudid.

"If you don't sleep and rest, you aren't going to heal," he explained kindly as I cried in my hospital bed. "You need this."

My pain had gone from a three on a one to ten scale up to a twelve that night. It was unbearable. I allowed the nurse to add the Dilaudid to my IV, and I slept for the first time in three days. In the morning, I wanted more.

"Do you want some more Dilaudid?" the nurse asked me.

"Yes," I said immediately. I just wanted to go back to sleep again and wake up when I was ready to go home. "I mean *no!*" I added quickly. I did want it, but I was not going to take it. One dose was all I needed. I called several of my sober supports, crying. "I had to take a dose of Dilaudid," I told them one by one. "The surgeon insisted."

"That's perfectly fine, Mallory," my sober friend Lisa told me when she came to visit that morning. "When I had my boobs done, I had to take opiates for days."

Another sober support came by. "Don't worry, Mallory," he said. "When I had surgery, I was on a morphine drip. I pumped it all day long."

I was disappointed in myself and felt depressed. This is what drugs did to me. No matter what, I was not going to take any more. I left the hospital without any prescriptions.

At almost five years sober I saw a doctor about a problem that I've been having with my jaw.

"I want you on a muscle relaxer," he said.

"I'm in recovery. I already told you that." *What is wrong with this guy?* I wondered. *Is he deaf or just completely ignorant?*

"You need a muscle relaxant," he insisted. "This problem is not going to resolve without one."

I googled the meds that he suggested and showed him that they are not recommended for people in recovery.

"Why are you upset?" he asked me after a fifteen-minute debate.

"I told you that I'm in recovery," I said for the umpteenth time. "I am not taking a muscle relaxer."

His written report stated that I refused muscle relaxers due to their addictive qualities and that I had not agreed to his suggested treatment.

Two days later, at our weekly house meeting, I shared this story with my residents.

"Our house manager and I were both told to take medications in the past three weeks that are not allowed in recovery. Each of us needs to own our choices when it comes to medication. Just because a doctor prescribes something doesn't mean that it's okay for us."

We went on to talk about how we feel that doctors, dentists, and nurses should all be required to learn about addiction during their schooling. They should be asking us if we're in recovery, but until the day when they do, we will keep telling them—at least those of us who truly want to be sober.

Heads nodded all around the room. My residents began raising their hands to share similar stories that had happened to them. Addicts and alcoholics are not like the average population. We have a disease of the brain that makes it impossible for us to safely use medications that nonaddicted people can. No laughing gas at the dentist, no sips of champagne at weddings, no bottles of pain pills sitting in our medicine cabinets "just in case"—no Ambien or Xanax on overseas flights.

Anything mood or mind-altering can bring us right back to where we started—or worse. Nonalcoholic beer has alcohol in it. I have spoken to numerous people who relapsed by starting there, feeling like they were drinking socially but thinking they were safe. They weren't.

Today, Tylenol or Advil work just fine for me, and I don't even like to take these. Given the choice, I'll go to a fresh juice bar and drink a shot of turmeric any day.

If It's Broken, We Will Fix It

Since opening my first house, the more damaged a resident is, the harder I try to love and help her. Most of the women arrive with a story to explain their disease.

"I started drinking because—'my husband cheated on me with his yoga teacher,' 'my son died in a car crash,' 'I was molested as a child,' 'I was sick and needed surgery,' 'my mother died,' 'my father died,' 'I lost my job'"—the list goes on and on. I understand, because I used to write the script myself. *I was a single mother; my mother and grandmother were alcoholics; I was anxious, lonely, tired; my parents didn't understand me.* I told myself all these things and more every time I poured a drink or snorted a line of coke. For me, those circumstances and stories just fueled my disease, providing an excuse for my excesses. It's hard to tell what comes first—the trauma or the disease. Regardless, staying stuck in our pasts can keep us sick. There is nothing that drinking or drugging will make better.

"Your way hasn't worked so far," I often said. "Why don't you try being sober for a little while? You can always go back out if you want to. Alcohol and drugs aren't going anywhere."

I have had women on walkers, only recently graduating from wheelchairs. One was in her early twenties. We gave these women chores that they can handle, hugged them often, and tried to help them do things that many take for granted. Sometimes they let us help, but the more they healed, the harder they tried to be independent, even if a simple task could be completed in half the time by someone else. Some days I rubbed their feet, necks, and shoulders while they moaned about the difficulty they were having with walking, fatigue, and pain. Touch can be comforting and restorative. In our addictions, many of us shunned human contact.

We have had many residents who lost their partners to overdose right in front of their eyes. We meet with them often. We listen to them. We wipe their tears away. We hug them. My goal is to help them move forward and work through their grief sober. Sometimes they need trauma counseling, and we encourage them to get it.

"You're here for a reason," I tell each one of them. "I don't know why we lived, while so many others died, but we are blessed."

I remind myself of this every day as soon as I wake up. I believe that we can work through anything if we work on our program and don't drink or drug. Some days are easier than others. When someone feels particularly awful, I suggest that she do something special for herself today—take a bubble bath, swim in the ocean, watch a movie, attend a yoga class. Most of all, I suggest that she reach out to someone else who is sick and suffering.

"It's not all about us," I remind them.

"For me," I tell my women, "asking another alcoholic how she's doing today takes the focus off me and allows me to think about someone other than myself. Honestly, I'm sick of talking about myself. Before I know it, my own problems don't seem that important, and I've been able to help someone else."

Many of my residents have tried to hurt or kill themselves. "Suicide is a permanent solution to a temporary problem," I remind them. I share stories with them of how I, too, didn't want to wake up some days, but today I wake up with joy and gratitude. I want to spread those feelings.

A resident called Daphne hoarded her sleep meds for several days and then took a large dose at once. She woke in the morning surprised. "I was hoping I wouldn't wake up again," she told me. Eighteen years old—most of her life still ahead of her—but the things she had experienced in those years were so awful that she wanted to die.

"Come here," I said, opening my arms.

She came closer, and I wrapped her tight, putting love from my heart into hers.

"You're worth it," I whispered in her ear. "It might not feel like it right now, but you have everything ahead of you."

We pulled apart, and she was sobbing. Her long reddish hair was beautiful, her skin clear, her lips full and pouting.

"It's going to be okay," I promised her.

I called Daphne's family and treatment team immediately. She went for a psychiatric assessment and was later picked up to go back to treatment. Drugs and alcohol are just a symptom, we are told. Sometimes people need more help than a transitional home provides.

"I love you," I told her as she was leaving with all her belongings, lugging big black trash bags out to the driveway. "I hope you can come back soon."

"I love you too," she said.

Julia smiled and told me she was doing great whenever I saw her. A mom of three, her *baby daddy* had moved on to someone else. Heartsick, she turned to drugs. As soon as I left, she called her family, crying for hours. The other residents told me that Julia was putting on a show for me. All she wanted was to get this guy back, and he was not interested.

"Julia," I told her, sitting beside her bed, "what's going on? You keep telling me you're fine, and then I'm told that you're crying for hours on the phone and telling everyone that you want your ex back."

"I do," she admitted. "I just can't get over it."

"But he cheated on you," I reminded her. "He doesn't want to be with you. You deserve to be with someone who loves and values you."

"I want him," she said, bursting into tears. "I only want him!"

Little bloody lines were running along her inner arm. They were small and straight.

"Have you been cutting yourself?"

"Just yesterday."

"You're not allowed to cut yourself here. Did you use a razor?" Straight razors were also not permitted on property.

"No."

"So what did you cut yourself with?"

"A kitchen knife."

I felt sick. This poor woman had gone into the kitchen and taken a knife into her room to cut herself. She needed to feel some real pain to deal with her emotional turmoil. The drugs were gone and hurting herself was taking their place.

"You can't cut yourself, Julia. I'm going to have to call your therapist and your family and tell them."

"I know," she said, looking relieved.

The next day, while we were waiting for her trauma team to pick her up for additional inpatient treatment, Julia went outside to smoke a cigarette. I waited inside the house for her ride to arrive.

"Julia's burning herself!" one of the other residents yelled, running into the house from the backyard.

I ran outside, and Julia was burning small round holes into her hand, holding the lit end of her cigarette up to her skin until the pain was unbearable.

"Give me that!" I grabbed the cigarette from her hand and extinguished it quickly. "Let's clean you up," I told her, leading her inside by the unburned hand. "You're going to be okay."

Other women turn to food after they put down their beloved drugs. It has not been unusual for me to house women who have gained thirty, forty, a hundred, even a hundred and fifty pounds. They arrive looking miserable, but all they want is a ride to a fast-food chain and a supermarket. They pile their carts up with Coke, chips, candy, frozen meals, macaroni and cheese.

"How about something healthy?" I suggested. "These blueberries look really good."

"I hate blueberries!" Patty told me. Patty had just come from inpatient where she had gained thirty pounds in as many days, blaming it on their caterer.

"Have you ever tried making a smoothie with ice, blueberries, a little banana, some almond milk?" I asked her.

"That's nasty," she said, stuffing some Doritos into her cart. She headed to the cookie section for Oreos.

"Do you know that Oreos have been proven to be as addictive as cocaine?" I asked her.

"I believe it," she said, laughing. "I love them!"

I brought my sober nutritionist over the following week. She was young and beautiful, bursting with energy and positivity.

"These smoothies are so healthy and delicious," she told the women. "I like to put some chia and flaxseeds in mine for extra energy."

The residents gathered around, seemingly interested, some of them asking questions. Could they add strawberries? Yogurt?

"You can add anything," the nutritionist told them. "They're so yummy."

She poured small cups of the smoothies and passed them around. Patty was sitting on the couch, her back to the kitchen.

"Patty," I said, walking over to her, "don't you want to taste the smoothies?"

"No. I told you I don't drink those." A can of Coke sat in front of her.

She was typing madly on her phone and wouldn't look at me. She refused to taste the smoothies or to engage in the session at all. Patty had gained over a hundred pounds over the past two years. Her feet and ankles were so swollen that she could barely walk, and she was only twenty-two. A few minutes later, I received a phone call from her mother.

"Patty is hysterical," she said. "She thinks you brought the nutritionist over just for her."

"There are lots of other residents here who wanted the nutritionist to come. She has helped me tremendously with *my* diet."

"I know that, but she doesn't believe me."

As soon as the nutritionist was gone, Patty lumbered into the kitchen to make herself a second breakfast. It was 10:15 a.m. She toasted four slices of Wonder bread and slathered them with butter. Half a pound of bacon was cooking in the microwave, and she stuffed it inside the bread when it was done, devouring the two sandwiches in minutes. The drugs were gone for now, but food had replaced them. Something would need to change if Patty was going to heal.

Eating in bedrooms is not allowed, but I find crumpled candy wrappers and cold McDonald's fries under residents' beds. When we make a trip to Starbucks, I pick up an iced coffee with soy milk, while a large Frappuccino is their drink of choice. Wherever calories, fat, and sugar hide, my large women find them. I understand, and my heart goes out to them. Consuming these foods and beverages gives them temporary comfort, but then they hate themselves because they look and feel terrible.

I encourage swimming, yoga, walking on the beach. I offer discounted memberships to a nearby gym. I exercise every single day, and they see me in my running and spin clothes, my yoga and tennis outfits. The sugary candy that

I ate every single day for the first two months of my recovery has been replaced with Greek yogurt, fresh fruit, green juice, lean fish, and chicken. I feel better when I eat clean and exercise, and I try to lead by example. Sometimes it helps.

I have learned to focus on my insides today. Through a lot of hard work, I began to focus on others, and to care less about the way I appeared. *What other people think of me is none of my business,* I remind myself often. I don't want a face that doesn't match my arms and legs. I'm getting older, and I'm grateful for that every day.

Before I got sober, I visited numerous plastic surgeon's offices in Manhattan. I took off my clothes and stood before them.

"What brings you in today?" they asked me.

"What do you think I need?" I answered. "You're the expert."

For years, I explored breast lifts and augmentation, a butt lift, a face-lift, eyelid surgery, a brow lift, a mini face-lift, laser treatments, a neck job. I was poked with needles and had my eyes done at the age of thirty-nine.

Today, I'm older, and I look it. I'm sober, and I have learned to love and accept myself the way I am. I watch my residents going for lip injections, Botox, Juvederm, Restylane, laser, hair extensions—the list goes on and on. Their eyebrows pull up unevenly; they have scars under their clothing from prior surgeries; their lips pout out unnaturally, their faces are black and blue.

Some of my broken girls have moved out and have gone on to have healthy relationships. They have gone back to school, started new careers, or reentered the workplace. They have mended relationships with their families, had babies, been reunited with the children they had lost to their disease.

"You're beautiful just the way you are," I remind them.

If you're broken, come to us. We will love you until you can love yourself.

Epilogue

Maybe There *Were* Warning Signs

Addiction is the great rationalizer. As addicts and alcoholics, we explain our behaviors away and are often able to hide them well—until we no longer can. The Big Book says that alcoholics are typically highly intelligent and successful, and our disease centers in the mind as well as the body. Once we understand that we have a disease and an allergy to alcohol and drugs, our mental obsession still lingers on, trying to convince us that we are cured now and we can have just one drink on vacation, or we can now control our drug use again. For many of us, the obsession never lifts completely.

Two years after I got sober, I was flying to Boston with Mark to visit Jack at college. It was an early-morning flight, and for two and a half hours I obsessed about having a drink with dinner that night. Mark had booked a table at a steak house, and the image of a big glass of full-bodied red wine would not leave my consciousness. *I could probably have one glass of wine tonight,* I kept thinking. *Nobody knows me in Boston, and I wouldn't have to tell anybody. I haven't had a drink in two years, and I don't know anybody who sells coke in Boston, so I don't have to worry about doing that. Coke was really my problem, not alcohol. I was never an alcoholic.*

In the cab on the way to our hotel, I told Mark that I was thinking of having a glass of red wine at dinner that night.

"Why would you do that?" he asked. *Clearly he didn't understand the mind of an alcoholic.*

"I need to get to an A.A. meeting right away," I told him.

We checked into the hotel, and I walked over to a mid-day meeting. If I could share with other alcoholics that I was craving a drink in Boston, I knew that the craving would pass. It was a round robin, and the chair chose someone across the circle from me. After about five shares, I realized that I would not have a chance to speak. I left the meeting dejected, still thinking about that glass of wine. The craving had lasted for almost six hours already, and it wasn't subsiding. As I walked back toward our hotel, I called my sponsor Sharon—the call went right into her voice mail. I couldn't get a break. I called Al next, and he answered right away.

"Thank God you answered!" I exclaimed.

"What's up, baby girl?" he asked. "How's Boston?"

Within ten minutes the craving had completely passed. Al told me that it was completely normal for me to be thinking of drinking in Boston—I was an alcoholic, wasn't I? We were both laughing by the end of the call. I had struggled for hours, but simply sharing my craving with another alcoholic in recovery had reminded me of where that one drink would take me. Mark and I had a great weekend with Jack. I drank Pellegrino with lemon and lime at dinner that night and ate a small piece of chocolate cake. Occasionally, even a healthy eater needs a reward, and if it's chocolate versus a drink, chocolate will win every time.

I have watched many people die from this disease since I got sober. Recently, a young woman named Lizzie, with whom I became friendly when I moved to Florida, passed away at the age of thirty-two. She was a beautiful person who had come down to Florida to get sober when she was twenty-seven. Her drugs of choice were cocaine and Xanax.

Two years ago, she told me sadly that she had started drinking socially again.

"I only have one or two," she explained. Her beautiful face, usually covered with a big smile, looked sad.

"Why are you drinking if you feel badly about it?" I asked her.

She had been sober for three years and walked away from her sponsor and meetings when her life started to get good again. She had a career that she loved and a boyfriend that she believed was the man she would spend her life with.

"I just am," she said. "And I feel weird about telling people in the program."

"You can always talk to me about it," I told her. "I'm not going to judge you. You know that the program is here for you if you want to come back."

"I know," she said.

Lizzie drank socially for two years. The last time I saw her I asked her how things were going. She was having problems with her boyfriend, and she had gotten very drunk at a party recently.

"I felt like crap the next day," she told me. "I'm only drinking one or two again."

"No drugs?" I asked her.

"No way!" she said, looking at me directly with her big blue eyes. "The stuff down here is crap. It wouldn't be worth it."

"People are dying everywhere. Drugs are being cut with Fentanyl and other stuff that kills you. It's on the news all the time."

Lizzie's boyfriend found her dead in their bedroom. There was cocaine and Xanax on her bedside table. One or two drinks had finally taken her back to her drugs of choice. Hundreds of people have mourned her. She was a loving and caring person, taken way too soon.

This is just one example of how our disease works to kill us. It wants us drinking, taking drugs, and ultimately dead. The only known cure is the 12-step program, which is why I work it every day. I know that my addiction will try to convince me that I can have one frozen margarita with salt while on vacation, or one glass of red wine when I'm dining out with nonalcoholic friends or family. One drink is too many, we are reminded, and a hundred are never enough.

Smoking pot is a great example of how unmanageable my drug use was, even though I believed that cocaine was my only problem. As an adult, smoking weed almost always made me faint, but that didn't stop me from smoking it again and again. I went to the off-Broadway show *The Marijuana-Logues* one night. It was a show about three stoners who sat on the stage making jokes about smoking weed the entire time. It was hysterical, and I left there feeling like it would have been even funnier if I were stoned when I had seen it. The three actors seemed stoned during the show, and I wanted to watch it again under the influence.

I bought tickets to see it a second time and took a date. Right before entering the theatre, I smoked two hits of pot. It was a freezing cold night—January in New York City, and as I walked the last block to the theatre, I felt like I was going to faint. "I think I'm going to faint," I told my date, who had also smoked with me. "I'm going to buy something with sugar in it to bring my blood sugar up." We walked into a deli where I bought a pack of Bubble Yum and some Skittles. I popped a handful of Skittles in my mouth, followed by a big wad of bubble gum. We walked to the theatre and got in line with our tickets. The next thing I remember, I was lying on the floor. I felt like I had died.

"Are you okay?" my date asked. "I was able to grab your head before it hit the floor." Someone had carried a chair into the lobby for me, and they helped me sit down.

"Here's some orange juice," the theatre employee told me, handing me a plastic cup filled with orange liquid.

"I don't like juice," I told him.

"Just drink it," my date said.

I didn't want empty calories, but I took a little sip of the orange juice. The show had already started, and I was unable to make it to our seats. I was so weak, and every time I tried to walk, I felt faint. I was in and out of consciousness. The theatre staff allowed us to sit near the exit. I sat through the entire show going in and out of a blackout. For me, *The Marijuana-Logues* was definitely better sober.

About six months later, I began dating Mark, and we flew out to Las Vegas for a short vacation. I purchased tickets for us to see Paul McCartney at the newly remodeled theatre the Joint at the Hard Rock. It was opening night for the theatre, and the tickets cost me seven hundred and fifty dollars. I was beyond excited to see the show and to share this gift with Mark.

We sunbathed most of the day by our hotel pool. The temperature was about a hundred and ten degrees, so we spent a lot of time in the pool, where I drank iced coffees to stave off my thirst. We had dinner at Nobu before the show, and I drank three glasses of white wine and ate some sushi.

Entering the theatre, we stood toward the stage—our tickets were standing room only, and we wanted a good view. As we waited for the show to begin, a guy pushed past us, and I smelled some really good weed.

"Do you have any weed?" I asked him coyly.

"Yeah," he said. "Do you want a hit?" He was a big, burly guy, and he smiled and took out a small pipe and handed it to me. I took a hit and handed the pipe to Mark. The guy hid his pipe away again and walked up closer to the stage. I felt a nice buzz. A few minutes later, the weed guy walked back toward me again.

"Do you want another hit?" he asked graciously.

"Sure," I said, taking the proffered pipe again and inhaling deeply. Mark declined a second hit. Right as Paul McCartney was being introduced, I felt myself getting really dizzy.

"I'm really dizzy," I told Mark. "I feel like I'm going to faint." Mark and I were just getting to know each other, and he had never seen me faint before.

The next thing I remember, I was being carried through a hallway, approaching a set of stairs. A muscular man in a hotel uniform was holding my feet, and Mark was holding my shoulders. They carried me up three flights of stairs in an otherwise empty stairwell and took me into the nursing station. The nurses checked me out, and I insisted on going back downstairs to the concert. I didn't want Mark to miss the show because of me.

Mark led me back into the theatre. I was very weak, leaning against a wall. Paul was playing "Jet." He looked adorable. *He was still so thin and cool, even at his age.* I was happy that he had met a wonderful woman and married for the third time.

I came to and was in the stairwell again. The same man was holding my legs, and Mark was holding my shoulders. They took me back to the nursing station. This happened a third time. I was so tired and just couldn't make it through the concert. The nurses wanted me to go to the hospital. I had to be back in New York the next day to get my children from their dad, and there was no way I was going to the hospital. Mark and I had a very early flight the next morning, and I was afraid that we would miss it.

"Can I just lie down for a little while so my boyfriend can watch the show?" I asked the nurse. There was a cot in her room, and it looked so inviting to me. At that point it was as appealing as a Tempur-Pedic mattress covered in Frette linens with a down comforter.

"If you lie down, you have to go to the hospital," she insisted.

The nurses insisted that I sign a form stating that I refused to go to the hospital, and eventually Mark and I made our way to the hotel's exit. We had missed the entire show. Walking across the parking lot was not an easy feat for me, and it felt like it took us an hour to reach our rental car. I fell into a deep sleep as soon as we got into our room, and Mark checked me every few minutes to make sure I was breathing. I made it home the next day for my reunion with Morgan and Jack. Pot should have been a thing of the past for me by then, but that was not the last time that I smoked it.

I'm not sure why I kept thinking that I could smoke pot without fainting, but I kept trying. Mark and I went out to shoot pool with our friend Archie one night, and afterward, before going out to dinner, I asked Archie if he had any weed. We had been drinking cocktails at the pool hall, and I wanted something else. My coke dealer wasn't answering my texts, and my craving for drugs was whispering to me.

Archie and I had been friends for a long time, and he always had a stash of weed. We went to his apartment to smoke then walked to a nearby restaurant. There were stations there where you ordered salads, pastas, pizzas, and more, and I offered to order the salads. I was on line when I felt myself fainting. When I came to, I was lying on the floor once again, Mark and Archie helping me to our table.

Mark told me that someone had come over to him and asked, "Is that your wife on the floor over there?" (We were married by then.)

"Probably," Mark answered.

I literally lay on the banquette at our table while Archie and Mark ate dinner and had more drinks. I could barely talk, let alone move. *It's kind of amazing that Mark married me.*

Long before I began smoking pot and fainting I had another warning sign. I was in my mid-twenties and working in marketing at a popular women's clothing chain. We had an overnight conference in Connecticut, and I decided to buy some coke on my way up. I stopped at my dealer's apartment and got my coke and then began the drive up the FDR. I did a hit in each nostril. The next thing I knew, I was coming to behind the wheel of my car. I didn't understand what a blackout or a brownout was at the time, but I was clearly in one. I kept snorting more, thinking that more coke would wake me up. When I arrived at the hotel, I checked in and went downstairs to dinner with my colleagues. The entire evening, I was in and out of conversation. I would find myself in the middle of a discussion that I didn't remember starting.

Mid-meal, I went into the phone booth outside the dining room and called my dealer.

"Hey," I told him, "what is in this stuff? I keep going in and out of consciousness." My dealer at that time was a flamboyantly gay man who held nightly drug parties in his studio apartment on the Upper East Side.

"Oh, no, darling!" he said in his playful voice. "I must have given you the wrong thing!"

"What is it?" I asked.

"It must be K," he said. "I'm so sorry! I'll make it up to you the next time I see you."

I had no idea what K was but thought it might be a drug called Special K that I had heard people took at gay clubs. I have since learned that it is "ketamine," a prescription analgesic, which is often referred to as a "club drug." I don't understand why anyone would want to take it, but I finished mine off before the end of the conference and remembered almost nothing about the entire night or following day. A so-called normal person would not have continued to snort this substance once they realized that it wasn't what they wanted, but I didn't stop until it was gone.

From the time my children were young, I warned them of the dangers of drugs and alcohol. "Alcoholism and addiction run in our family," I told them over dinner sometimes. "You have to be very careful and never take cocaine or heroin, because those are very hard to stop."

Morgan and Jack would look at me patiently, humoring my warnings. I worried that they would get hooked on coke like I had, but I wasn't going to tell them that. They knew that my grandmother and mother had both been alcoholics, and there were some issues on their dad's side too. They were definitely at risk, and I wanted to protect them. Addiction is a family disease, and the majority of people with alcohol and drug problems report having others in their family who are also alcoholics or addicts.

So I guess there were warning signs long before my return to cocaine and my eventual admission of defeat. There are many more stories that I could share, but these are a few that stand out for me as I look back over my thirty-nine-year run. Since I got sober at the age of fifty-one, I sometimes think that in order for me to be sober for as long as I was drinking and using, I will have to reach the age of ninety without picking up a single drink or drug. I hope to be one of those old ladies sitting in the front of my daily A.A. meetings, sharing my experience, strength, and help with newcomers.

"Welcome," I will say, putting my wrinkly old arms around a newcomer. "I'm Mallory. I'm an alcoholic."

And today instead of saying "Don't worry, you can live at my house," I'm going to say, "Don't worry, you can live in one of my sober houses."

The End

About the Author

Mallory Neuberger was raised on Long Island and moved to Manhattan after finishing her MS in counseling psychology at the University of Pennsylvania. She raised her children, Morgan and Jack, in Tribeca and Soho and fell into her family history of addiction there where she ended up living a double life and wanting to die.

As a sober woman now, Mallory cannot find enough hours to do all the things she enjoys. These include playing tennis, practicing yoga, spending time with family and friends, hanging out on the beach and swimming in the ocean, reading avidly, listening to live music, traveling, and working with others in recovery.

After an unfulfilling but successful thirty-one-year career in marketing and then real estate, Mallory loves her work today, owning and running two women's sober houses. She lives in Delray Beach, Florida, with her husband, Mark, and their dachshunds, Grandpa and Cooper.

CPSIA information can be obtained
at www.ICGtesting.com
Printed in the USA
LVHW011337130519
617615LV00006B/587/P